14.95

TIGER WOODS
GOLFING CHAMPION

TIGER WOODS
GOLFING CHAMPION

By David R. Collins

Illustrated by Larry Nolte

PELICAN PUBLISHING COMPANY
Gretna 1999

The word "Pelican" and the depiction of a pelican are
trademarks of Pelican Publishing Company, Inc., and are registered
in the U.S. Patent and Trademark Office

Library of Congress Cataloging-in-Publication Data

Collins, David R.
    Tiger Woods, golfing champion / by David R. Collins ; illustrated
by Larry Nolte.
    p.   cm.
    Includes bibliographical references (p.) and index.
    Summary: Presents a biography of the professional golfer, who at
the age of twenty-one became the first person of color and the
youngest player to win the Masters Golf Tournament.
    ISBN 1-56554-322-X (hc : alk. paper)
    1. Woods, Tiger—Juvenile literature. 2. Golfers—United States—
Biography—Juvenile literature. [1. Woods, Tiger. 2. Golfers.
3. Racially mixed people—Biography.] I. Nolte, Larry, ill.
II Title.
GV964.W66C66 1998
796.352'092—dc21
[B]   98-14710
                                                  CIP
                                                  AC

Printed in the United States of America

Published by Pelican Publishing Company, Inc.
1000 Burmaster Street, Gretna, Louisiana 70053

Contents

Preface

Tiger Woods is special. Few people would argue with that statement. Yet trying to focus on exactly what makes him so unique is as challenging as trying to shoot a hole in one. A collection of high school juniors and seniors recently accepted that challenge by sharing their thoughts about what makes Tiger Woods special.

"He's so talented," offered one student. "He makes golf look like the easiest game to play—and he wins so many tournaments."

True enough. Tiger makes golf *look* easy. Whether he is driving, chipping, or putting, he hits that ball with complete poise and precision. His shots, long or short, are totally calculated and mapped out in his mind. He can send a ball sailing 350 yards, then minutes later tap in a four-foot putt. As for tournaments, he began winning international titles when he was eight, and he shows no signs of stopping. The youngest to win the prestigious Masters Tournament, he didn't just win it—he won it by an amazing twelve strokes!

"He's so young," another student commented. "He's like one of us."

Yes, Tiger is barely a man in the legal sense. He looks even younger when he's golfing because many of his competitors are considerably older. He's neat and stylish, displaying good manners and a warm smile. Tiger gives youth a good name. He doesn't stage wild temper tantrums or dye his hair green to gain the spotlight. He lets his talent speak for him on the golf course, and he mirrors that quality performance with modesty and eloquence when he is not playing.

"He's not ashamed to show love and respect for his parents and other adults," one student volunteered. The sight of Tiger Woods publicly hugging his dad and mom after a match has delighted millions. "I couldn't have done anything without them," he has openly admitted. "They have always been there for me." Tiger also speaks with appreciation for those great golfers who have preceded him on the links, especially minority figures who overcame special obstacles.

"He reaches out to others, sharing his talent and wealth," another high school junior stated. In January 1997 this golfing superstar started the Tiger Woods Foundation. Its goal is to help poor children, in this country and abroad, through golf. "Golf has allowed me to reach many of my dreams," Tiger said when announcing the foundation. "I'd like to help other young people reach their dreams too. A person can't just take. A person has to give back."

"Tiger won't let himself be labeled or used by anyone," another high-school student said.

That's very true. Tiger is part white, black, Asian and American Indian—and he is proud of every part. "But it is not your race or nationality that makes you what you are," Tiger said. "It is what you do with yourself."

Clearly, Tiger Woods has done plenty with himself. He has helped to lift a minor sport into a major sport through his golfing talent and his example as a sportsman. Dollarwise, sports officials estimate Tiger has had a $650 million impact on the golf world during his short time as a superstar. He casts a positive spotlight on youth, winning admirers not only for himself but for his entire age bracket. "My grandfather is always complaining about the younger generation being lazy and selfish," one junior girl confessed. "But even *he* likes Tiger Woods." He is his own person, not letting himself be used or claimed by others. He's worked hard for his success, yet he wants to share it with others.

Yes, Tiger Woods is special. High-school students know what sets him apart. He is a quality athlete. More importantly, he is a quality person.

TIGER WOODS
GOLFING CHAMPION

Chapter One

Swinging a Club

Eldrick.

It's an unusual name, isn't it? Eldrick. That name belonged to one of the world's greatest athletes, but he is known today as Tiger. Tiger Woods. The story behind his name is as extraordinary as the life he has led and the accomplishments he can claim.

Earl and Kultida Woods wondered if they might receive a special Christmas gift during December 1975. Their first baby was due to arrive late that month. Yet when Christmas came and went, relatives and friends wondered if the baby would make an entrance early in 1976.

But on December 30, 1975, just before the year ended, the Woods' infant made his appearance. He was a healthy and hearty child who announced his arrival with squeals and yells galore. Kultida, known as Tida, wanted a special name for her new son. Relying on her own creative imagination, the woman from faraway Thailand came up with the name of Eldrick.

Earl Woods accepted his wife's choice for their child's name, but he had his own ideas of what his son would be called. An Army man, Earl had served his country during the Vietnam War. A Green Beret, he was a soldier trained to carry out dangerous, top-secret missions. Earl was an expert with explosives, and he worked closely with top South Vietnamese officers on a variety of war assignments. Lt. Col. Nguyen Phong was a good friend, and more than once he saved Earl's life. To Earl, Nguyen was like a brave tiger, fearless when facing death. In honor of his fighting buddy, Earl began calling his newborn son "Tiger." The nickname stuck. On his twenty-first birthday, December 30, 1996, Tiger officially and legally dropped the name Eldrick once and for all.

Earl Woods brought more than memories of a best friend back when he returned from Vietnam. While working at an Army base in Bangkok, Thailand, he met a secretary named Kultida Punsawad. Although immediately attracted to Kultida, Woods proceeded cautiously in the relationship. One reason for his caution was age: He was thirty-seven, and she was twenty-three. Earl's first marriage produced three children but had ended in divorce. Woods did not want to get hurt again, and he did not want to hurt anyone else either.

Kultida was just as determined to be careful with any possible romance. Earl cut a handsome figure in a uniform, flashed a quick, friendly smile, and displayed a gentleman's manners. Still, when he asked Kultida out, the secretary used a custom familiar to young eligible females in her native country: She brought along a chaperone. Amused, Earl made the most of the situation, and his good nature impressed Kultida. She brought along no chaperones in the dates that followed, and in 1969 they were married.

Earl and Tida Woods headed to California, settling into Cypress, a suburb outside of Los Angeles. Retiring from the U.S. military after twenty years of service, Earl found work with an aviation and rocket-building company, McDonnell Douglas. His job was to get the best and safest materials for the lowest possible prices. It was a challenge, and Earl thrived on challenges.

However, the challenge he faced in his Cypress neighborhood was different. Despite all that had occurred in the United States in the 1960s to promote racial harmony, some people still nursed prejudice against minorities. Earl is a quarter American Indian, a quarter Chinese, and half black. His wife Tida is a quarter Chinese, a quarter white, and half Thai. Some people in the Woods' all-white neighborhood had little use for the newcomers. They showed their feelings by throwing garbage at the house and on the lawn and by driving by and yelling names. Some even fired shots at the house with BB guns.

If those neighbors thought their actions would cause Earl and Tida to pack their bags and move, they were totally wrong. The couple resolved to stick it out. No one was going to make them run. Both of them had seen the Vietnamese War up close. They had lost loved ones in bloody battles there. A few limes or eggs hurled at their house or a few BBs fired into the siding were not going to send the Woodses packing.

The attacks gradually stopped. Earl and Tida minded their own business, but they were always willing to share friendly chatter. They worked in their yard, keeping their property in tip-top shape. In time, more and more neighbors stopped by to visit a few minutes or to chat about politics, the weather, and sports.

Sports were a favorite topic for Earl, with baseball being his prime interest. He'd won all-state honors in Little League when he was growing up in Kansas, and when a teenager he was the first black athlete to win all-state recognition in American Legion ball. While attending Kansas State University, he had been the only black to play baseball in the entire conference. Being a top ballplayer wasn't easy, either. When he traveled with the team, he couldn't always eat in the same restaurants or sleep in the same motels as his friends. Jackie Robinson became the first black man to play in the National Baseball League in 1947, but black people on college teams still endured countless acts of discrimination. "You can't eat here, boy," Earl heard more than once in restaurants his college team visited. Or a hotel clerk would say, "You'll have to find a room somewhere else." Being a black person in the 1950s was not easy, but the baseball player from Kansas accepted the treatment. He simply wanted to play the game for his school. In Cypress Earl didn't talk much about his own sports career, but he could quote countless statistics about other players and teams when he talked with his neighbors there.

Golf captured the time and attention of many of Earl's friends. Earl had never played the game himself. When he was a kid, it was considered a sport for the rich and for white people. He was forty-two when he swung a golf club for the first time, only to be badly beaten by a military buddy. Earl Woods did not like losing. He got a set of golf clubs and secretly practiced every chance he could. At first Earl just wanted to play better, but he quickly realized that golf had a special hold over him. He was addicted to the game. In less than six weeks, he played another round of golf with the buddy who had beaten him. This time Earl was ready to show his skills. For eighteen holes he drove, chipped, and putted with care and precision. His defeated friend was flabbergasted.

Although Earl regretted not having played golf earlier, he was never one to look back. Instead, he made a personal promise to himself that if Tida and he had a child, that child—boy or girl—would at least be exposed to the sport early in life. Earl wanted his child to enjoy the outdoor adventure and the intense challenge that golf provided.

Then along came Tiger. From the moment he came home from the hospital, he displayed energy and constant movement. There were no long naps for this baby. Craving activity, he absorbed everything around him, and his gaze caught everything that was going on. It seemed only natural for Earl to carry the boy into the garage each day to watch him practice chipping golf balls into a net. Carefully packaged into a metal high chair, Tiger perched for hours. He watched ball after ball sail forward. When dinnertime came, Tiger did not want to eat, so Tida brought food to her son. Whenever Tiger moved his head to follow the movement of his father's ball, Tida shoved a spoonful of food into the boy's mouth.

Before long, Earl decided his young observer needed a special toy. His father neatly trimmed down a putter and presented it to his son. While other boys clutched teddy bears, young Tiger Woods dragged his putter with him even before he could walk. By the age of ten months, the boy was actually swinging his short club, just as he had seen his father do thousands of times in the garage.

One day after finishing practice, Earl plopped into a chair in the garage to relax. His eyes widened as he watched Tiger slip out of his high chair and climb down. The boy picked up his putter and wobbled over to some golf balls. Copying his father's movements, Tiger swung his putter. Sure enough, the first ball hit the net. And the second. And the third.

"Praise the Lord!" Earl exclaimed. He leapt from his seat and ran to get his wife. Tida could not believe her eyes either. Why, the child wasn't even a year old, barely able to stand, and he was pounding golf balls into a net. From that moment on, they had no doubt in their minds that their child was very special.

As for Tiger, he just smiled and kept swinging away.

Chapter Two
Onto the Green

Earl and Tida knew they had witnessed their young child doing something extraordinary. Not even a year old, he was able to stand, swing a golf club, and hit golf balls. Quite a feat! But had Tiger's actions come from his own desire to perform—or had he just watched his father so often his moves were total imitation? It was likely the latter, they thought. Still, Tiger's accomplishment was amazing, and Earl and Tida agreed to give their son every opportunity to develop his golf talents as he wished. If Tiger wanted to play golf, his parents would ensure that nothing would stand in his way.

Golf, however, wasn't going to be the total focus in Tiger's life. Both Earl and Tida wanted their son to learn to read and write, to understand and discover. Tida loved having Tiger curl up on her lap as she shared the delightful adventures within a Doctor Seuss book. Tiger drew pictures and colored them, memorized his ABCs, and learned to count to ten in seconds. Still, whatever he did, wherever he went, the boy carried his putter with him.

Most parents would not think of taking a kid in diapers onto a golf course. But a father like Earl Woods would—and he did! Most bystanders merely chuckled at the sight—until they watched the kid swing a club. He could not use regular golf clubs because they were taller than he

19

was, but the way he handled the sawed-off set he had caused people to shake their heads in wonder.

Word spread about the amazing young kid who dazzled observers on the golf course. When television talk-show host Mike Douglas heard about Tiger, he invited him to be on his program. Earl and Tida agreed, hopeful that the crowd and bright lights would not overwhelm their two-year-old son. Tida put together a personal golf bag for Tiger and bought him a new pair of sneakers. A red and white shirt, khaki shorts, and a snappy red cap completed his ensemble.

Tiger shared the spotlight that day with two giants of entertainment: movie stars Jimmy Stewart and Bob Hope. Hope also was known as a dedicated amateur golfer, and a small artificial turf had been set up onstage for some good-natured competition. When Tiger drove a few shots off the green, Hope's eyebrows rose. A legendary comedian, he couldn't resist challenging the toddler to a putting contest.

"You got any money, kid?" Hope joked, hinting they might bet on the next shot. The audience roared with laughter.

Young Tiger had no idea what Bob Hope meant or why the people were laughing. Nevertheless, without saying a word, the boy went to his ball, placed it closer to the hole, and tapped it in.

The crowd laughed and applauded. Knowing he had been outdone by a two-year-old, Hope just shook his head. "If he doesn't make it as a golfer, he'll make it as a stand-up comic," the veteran performer quipped.

It was clear very early on that Tiger loved golf more then anything. That was just fine with Earl. Golf was something the two of them could share as father and son. Tida certainly had her place in the loving family picture, but Earl saw golf as a special bond he and Tiger could share.

The U.S. Navy Golf Course in Cypress became a second home to Earl and Tiger. It also became a school to the boy.

He learned that golf had its own vocabulary. Green was just a color to most three-year-olds, but to young Tiger Woods, it was the putting area of short grass around a hole on a golf course. To most kids Tiger's age, "eighteen" was just another number between one and twenty. To Tiger, it was the number of holes on a golf course, each broken down into a tee-off area, a fairway, and a putting green. The boy quickly learned how to score the game, keeping track of how many shots it took to get the ball in the hole after teeing off. The golfer using the fewest number of shots was the winner. Tiger listened to golfers talk and watched the way they drove and putted the ball. He absorbed the game like a golf green soaks up a summer shower.

Earl was careful not to push the game too hard. He loved golf, but he loved his son much more. He would not demand that Tiger practice and play if the boy did not want to.

But Tiger *did* want to. He frequently called Earl at work to ask if they could practice golf together. Earl would deliberately pause on the phone, keeping his son in suspense, before answering. Then he would agree, as he intended to do all along. Tida played the vital supporting role of taking Tiger to the golf course, where Earl was always waiting. Father and son would practice swings a bit and then head to the pitching area to hit balls. Tiger could not hit his balls far, but he developed his eye and body coordination. Then the pair would move on to the putting green. Putting placed the boy and his father on more equal footing. For hours the two would putt, carefully tapping theirs balls into the cup. They often challenged each other, with Earl occasionally letting his son win. To this day, Tiger claims he won many of those challenges on his own, fair and square!

Before long Earl was taking Tiger to play nine holes on the golf course, half the usual distance. The boy was given a tee to hit off of for each shot. People still talk about three-year-old Tiger shooting a 48 for nine holes at the U.S. Navy Course at Cypress.

"The kid swung a club better than most adults," said one observer. "Most kids that age would have been lucky to hit the ball at all. But Tiger had concentration and coordination far beyond his years. It was quite a sight to see, that's for sure."

Also quite a sight to see one day was young Tiger hitting his ball into a sand trap. Realizing he had to go to the bathroom, Tiger simply "pulled his pants down and went pee-pee. Then he pulled his pants up and hit the shot," Tida recalled. Nothing, not even nature, was going to stop the determined boy from playing his game.

Earl thought it was important that Tiger have a good SOP, or "Standard Operating Procedure." It was a military routine that Earl had learned well, and he believed it applied to golf too. SOP means that every time you perform a certain action or routine, you prepare for it in the same way, doing everything consistently. If you are going to fire a gun, you make certain the gun is in perfect condition for firing. You practice proper procedures for handling and aiming the gun before shooting. You need to be ready before you actually shoot.

Earl insisted that Tiger develop a pre-shot procedure, whether teeing off, driving, or putting. Any shot, according to Earl Woods, began *behind* the ball. The golfer first must see the target, then consider everything needed to reach the target, including distance, wind, and obstacles such as ponds, trees, and sand traps. So much needed to be considered even before choosing the right golf club, Earl told Tiger.

At first, Tiger did not like the SOP. He was eager to hit the ball right away. Over time, however, his father's advice gradually became part of the boy's approach to the game. And with that acceptance, Earl Woods felt a special bond

growing. He and his son had always enjoyed a loving relationship, but now they shared friendship too.

That friendship also was based on constant encourage-
ment. Tiger indeed made mistakes. When he swung, sometimes his balls glanced off of trees, plopped into ponds, or
sometimes just sat on the tee while a small clump of green
sailed into the air. But Tiger never heard any name-calling
from his father when he did. Earl never used words like
"failure." "Good shot!" and "Nice swing!" gave support to
the boy's efforts. The compliments quickly brought appre-
ciative smiles to Tiger's face.

By the time Tiger was four, Earl thought his son was
ready to compete against other golfers. Tiger was eager
too, but there were no tournaments for his age bracket.
The youngest divisions attracted ten- and eleven-year-old
golfers. A four-year-old entry? Tournament directors simply
laughed.

But in 1979, one local director agreed to give Tiger a
chance. The young boy had captured many people's attention, not merely as a novelty but as a serious golfer.
Contestants had to display three different golfing skills:
pitching, putting, and driving. A pitch shot is one in which
the golfer hits the ball high in the air only a short distance,
with a minimum of rolling upon landing. Putting requires
focused hitting of the ball into the hole from a nearby position on the green. Driving allows the golfer to hit the ball
a longer distance, hoping to land the ball as close to the
hole as possible.

Most of the contestants in the tournament were ten- and
eleven-year-olds. They no doubt sneered and snickered
when they heard about a four-year-old trying to challenge
them. But young Tiger soon erased those sneers and snick-
ers when he performed. He had perfected his SOP and
applied it. The onlookers had no idea how the young boy was
doing what he was doing. Eyes widened as he swung his club
and the ball sailed or edged its way toward its destination.

Unbelievable! Most people shook their heads in amazement, but two heads wore knowing and proud smiles: Earl and Tida Woods knew what their son could do. The only help he needed was getting the second-place trophy home! The handsome reward stood as tall as Tiger's shoulders.

Practice after practice, Tiger never got tired of playing golf. But Tida and Earl knew their son would be expected to know numbers other than those found on a golf scorecard. The parents drew up a 3" x 5" set of addition, subtraction, multiplication, and division cards. Tida gently but firmly drilled the numbers and problems into Tiger's head. They talked about stories in literature too, and the wonders of nature and ideas of people. Only after Tiger learned his lessons was he allowed to play golf.

That's Incredible was a popular television show in 1980, and Tiger's golfing talents earned him an invitation to appear. Both his cheerful smile and his stroking skills won over the audience. "When I get big," he declared, "I'm going to be Jack Nicklaus and Tom Watson." Nicklaus and Watson were two of the top golfers at the time. When new fans asked Tiger for his autograph, he had to take his time. He hadn't yet learned to write in script. Slowly and carefully, he printed his name.

When Tiger was five, he was notified that he could no longer play at the U.S. Navy Course in Cypress. A club rule supposedly prohibited anyone under the age of ten from playing on the course. Why had he been allowed to play there before? Earl Woods was pretty sure he knew the real reason: Tiger wasn't white like the rest of the members. Earl himself was called "Sergeant Brown" because of his color. So be it, Earl decided. They would find another place to play.

At nearby Heartwell Park Golf Club, Tiger impressed the club pro, Rudy Duran. Tiger stood only three feet, seven inches tall, but he played like a miniature professional golfer. Although he had his own personal style and stance, Tiger executed his golf swing with ease. He was focused, truly focused, on every aspect of his game. "I knew he could be something special," Duran said. "Actually, he already was."

Tiger felt at home at the new golf course right away. He liked his new coach, too. The boy had been spared being told about the possible discrimination at the U.S. Navy Golf Course.

But soon Tiger would face racial prejudice head-on. It would be an event that he would never forget.

Chapter Three
Into the Classroom

Tiger Woods could not wait to enter kindergarten in the fall of 1981. He was eager to show off his reading and writing skills and his talents for adding and subtracting. Being with older kids did not bother him at all. For two years he had been traveling around California, playing in tournaments—and winning his share, too. Even against boys several years older, Tiger proved himself a strong competitor.

Like everyone else, Tiger sported a new outfit for school on his first day. It didn't stay that way long. When he arrived at school, a group of sixth-graders decided to show him what they thought of a black boy coming to their school. They jumped on Tiger, beat him up, tied him to a tree, and printed a racial slur across the front of his new shirt. They proudly strutted off, calling him names and throwing rocks back at him. Tiger stood against the tree, confused and crying. Why would they do that? he wondered. He did not know any of the boys. He hadn't said or done anything to them.

The boys who hurt Tiger that day were caught and disciplined, but he never forgot the incident. It was the first time he was aware that his skin color made him different. It would not be the last time.

Inside the kindergarten classroom, Tiger impressed his teacher. He was always wide-awake and ready to work when he came to school. Perhaps getting up at four in the morning to get to golf tournaments helped establish that trait. He was always organized with his materials. That preparedness may have come from playing golf, too. Tiger once forgot to put his golf clubs in the trunk of the car. When he and his father arrived at the course, Tiger realized his mistake. The boy was devastated. Thankfully, Earl had seen the forgotten clubs and hid them in the back seat. Tiger was delighted, and the experience left him with the lesson to be prepared at all times.

Tiger's kindergarten teacher suggested he could move right into first grade. Tida and Earl Woods were proud of their son, but they were not about to make the decision without his help. "It's Tiger's life, not ours," his father always insisted. The decision was easy for Tiger. Playing in golf tournaments always put him with kids far older than he was. This time he wanted to stay with classmates his own age.

Because schoolwork came easily to Tiger, he could focus more on his golf game. Earl Woods decided to sharpen that focus—in a most unusual way. It was one thing to develop the physical skills of the game; it also was essential to develop the best mental attitude possible. Tiger was doing that too, but Earl Woods decided to sharpen that focus. After all, many people shared the idea that golf was 10 percent physical and 90 percent mental. Earl Woods was one of those people.

Earl Woods knew that golf is a game of good manners and sportsmanship. Yet he decided to toss all the courtesies aside to make Tiger mentally tough for any situation. When they arrived at the golf course, Earl applied a new strategy.

As Tiger prepared to tee off, Earl coughed or started talking.

When Tiger started to putt, Earl made birdcalls.

"Better watch out for that sand trap!" Earl yelled right before Tiger was ready to chip around the obstacle.

Tiger's eyes glared in anger. His whole body tensed in frustration. His father pulled every nasty and obnoxious trick he could think of to distract Tiger. At first, it worked: Tiger *did* lose his concentration. All he could think of was how disgusting the whole situation was. He wanted to play golf, not silly games.

Yet slowly, ever so slowly, his power of concentration strengthened. His father explained that whatever happened while Tiger was playing, he *had* to ignore outside distractions. People nearby were not always going to remain totally silent or totally still while Tiger golfed. Earl told his son that he must always stay completely focused on his game.

Tiger got the picture. While Earl tossed balls on the green and made bird sounds, Tiger ignored him. The young golfer did not even glance over when his father started sneezing or wheezing. The boy focused only on his golf game and nothing else around him. Sure enough, his game improved.

"Golf is a game where body and mind must work together," Earl kept telling his young son. "Physically, every movement of your body must be perfect; your arms, legs, shoulders, feet, head must be precisely and perfectly placed. Mentally, your thoughts must be given totally to your game while you are playing, nothing else."

Earl knew the value of keeping Tiger "psyched up" for golf off the course, too. The special tapes he bought for his son to listen to pounded subliminal positive messages into his mind. Immersed in the soothing, restful sounds of waves rolling against the shore or winds dancing among the trees were inspirational messages such as "I can do *anything* if I try!" or "I will my own destiny." Tiger carried the tapes around with him, playing them while he read in his room or practiced hitting in the garage. Listening to the tapes with their upbeat phrases gave Tiger confidence and support.

"People think we may have pushed Tiger too hard towards golf when he was growing up," Earl said. "But it was his choice, his desire. If ever he'd have said, 'I don't want to play anymore,' we would have stopped. But Tiger loved the game like I did—even more."

Rudy Duran loved working with Tiger. The boy's form was instinctively smooth, his strokes direct and powerful, his eye for the ball and its target always focused. In Rudy's opinion, young Tiger was like "a shrunken touring pro."

Still, Rudy saw no reason for young Tiger to have a one iron among his set of sawed-off clubs. It was the hardest club to hit with. A golfer Tiger's size certainly couldn't get up enough club speed to send a golf ball into the air. The club was as tall as he was!

"But I want one," Tiger insisted.

The next time Tiger, Earl, and Rudy were together, the boy slipped a one iron out of his father's bag. He swung and the ball went sailing, a near-perfect shot. Tiger managed to earn a one-iron club by proving he could use it well.

Most six- and seven-year-old kids seldom stay interested in anything for any length of time. They might play at a game for half an hour, maybe an hour at most. Tiger was different. He could stay on a golf course for hours, driving or putting, without getting bored. With Tiger constantly talking about golf, practicing golf, watching golf tournaments on television, and playing in them in real life, even Earl worried about his son being totally consumed by the sport. "Life is more than golf," Earl told his son. "I want you to have fun." Tiger just smiled. "This is how I have fun, Dad. This is the greatest fun in the world," Tiger said. Earl was satisfied. As long as Tiger enjoyed his world of golf, then it was OK.

Tida set down special rules, too—and she enforced them. Before Tiger could lift a golf club at home, he had to have his homework done. No sneaking off to the garage for a little chipping practice until the theme was written. No putting on the living-room carpet until the math problems were solved. Responsibility was drilled into young Tiger.

Tida also demanded the best manners on the golf course. Whether he was playing for fun or competing in a tournament, Tiger was expected to behave. When he didn't, Tida stepped in.

Once, when he was about six years old, Tiger blew an easy putt. In disgust, he slammed his club against his golf bag. A familiar voice rang out: "Penalize that boy!"

Tiger whizzed around. He knew who was shouting and he could not believe his ears. Tida's eyes flashed her anger. "Penalize that boy!" she told the tournament director. "Add a couple strokes to his score."

"Mom!"

"Be quiet! That bag didn't move. The golf club didn't make the mistake. Who made the bad shot?"

It was true, and Tiger knew it. He was to blame, not his golf bag or his golf club. If he made a mistake, he would have to pay the consequences. Both Tida and Earl Woods wanted their son to be the best golfer he could be, and they demanded the best behavior from him when he played. Tida was especially outraged at the antics and language of tennis stars like Jimmy Connors and John McEnroe, who challenged officials and threw temper tantrums. She sometimes even turned off the television set in disgust.

"You'll be a gentleman when you play," Tida often told Tiger. "I'll have no one saying I raised a spoiled child."

When Tiger wasn't competing in a weekend golf tournament in person, he took part in his own living room. The television set offered him a chance to watch other golfers, analyze their moves, and discuss the action with his father.

Both Tida and Earl kept close tabs on their son's wishes. If Tiger wanted to stop playing, they told him that would be just fine.

But it was just the opposite. Tiger loved the game. Whether practicing or competing, he could not get enough of golf. More and more trophies found their way into the Woods home.

When he was eight, Tiger got his first taste of world competition. He entered the Optimist International Golf Junior Championship. All of his opponents were older, and many showed their nervousness on the course. Earl was a bit nervous himself, worrying that perhaps Tiger was too young to compete. "Just have fun," Earl told his son. "It doesn't matter whether you win or lose."

Maybe it didn't matter to Earl, but it clearly mattered to Tiger. From the moment he teed off, his golf ball sailed exactly where he hoped it would go. Drives, chip shots, putts—all had the people in the gallery shaking their heads in disbelief. Tiger played not only with accuracy and skill but with total calm and concentration. He won the tournament, much to everyone's surprise. Tiger smiled when the reporters asked him what he liked to do for fun. "Fun to me is shooting low scores when I play golf," he replied. It was not the cocky answer of an arrogant eight-year-old; it was the honest answer of a dedicated young athlete. Earl Woods put aside his worries about Tiger's attitude. What he lacked in years, the boy made up for in maturity. When he heard rumors floating around that he might have won the tournament just as a lucky fluke, Tiger went back to win the Optimist International title three more times.

Tiger liked other amusements, too. On weekends, he enjoyed tossing a football around with Earl, and they watched weekend ball games on television. Tiger mastered the lyrics to countless rap songs, and he loved the rapid reflexes and quick thinking required for video games. He made friends easily, and his classmates respected his mind and friendly personality.

Tida guided the religious aspects of the Woods household, sharing the Buddhism of her native Thailand with Tiger. A Buddhist assumes responsibility for his own actions, never passing the blame to others for mistakes or misdeeds. Her religious beliefs were exactly why Tida would not let Tiger kick his golf bag, throw a club, or use bad language like other golfers. Respect for people is a key ingredient of the religion, as is the discipline of hard work toward any challenge. Even as a young boy, Tiger realized Buddhism fit a pattern for living he liked, and it fit his dreams as a golfer.

When he was nine, Tiger was watching television when a tragic story appeared on the news. In the faraway country of Ethiopia, countless numbers of African children were dying, the victims of starvation and disease. The more he watched, the sadder Tiger became. He knew he could be one of those children. Instead, he had loving parents, a good home and school, clothing, and plenty to eat every day. He also had a piggy bank in his bedroom, full of saved pennies, nickels, and dimes. Tiger carefully counted out twenty dollars and asked his mother to send it to the starving children in Ethiopia.

Earl and Tida Woods devoted themselves to their son. "Baby-sitter" was a word that was never used in the house. When invited to a party, either one of the parents would go—leaving the other at home. "I was very fortunate in that my parents always put my well-being above anything else," explains Tiger. "When I was growing up, there was always someone at home for me, someone I could share my problems with."

There would be much sharing in the next few years for Tiger Woods. There would be plenty of problems, too.

Chapter Four
Learning Big Lessons

"It's amazing how far and how hard this kid hits the ball," wrote a sports writer covering junior athletic standouts in the winter of 1985. "Tiger Woods is not much taller than most of his clubs, yet he handles them like they were born in his hands."

Actually, when Tiger was ten years old, he stood four feet, nine inches tall and weighed about eighty pounds. Yet he'd captured two Junior World Championship titles back to back, and Earl and Tida Woods were kept busy rearranging their furniture because of all the trophies Tiger was pulling in. "You just keep winning them," his father laughed. "We'll find the space."

But budgeting money to make sure Tiger got into the tournaments he needed and wanted to play was not easy. It didn't cost so much to play in the events sponsored by the California Junior Golf Association because they were close to home. What was expensive was getting to those competitions farther away, beyond California—even beyond the boundaries of the United States. Those were the tournaments that emptied the billfold fast. Canada, Mexico, France—yes, and even Thailand—all offered special opportunities and challenges. The family traveled together whenever they could. If it took more than one mortgage on the house, Earl would do it. If it took multiple credit-card charges, Earl would do it. Sacrifices could and would be made for Tiger. As long as the boy wanted to play golf and enter tournaments, there would be money for it. A newer car, a new outfit, new furniture—everything else could wait.

Tiger knew his parents were giving up things so that he could play in tournaments far away from home. He had plans, too, plans to somehow repay them in the future. "When I'm a pro, Daddy, do you think you could live on $100,000 a year?"

Earl laughed. "Let me think about that one," he answered. "The tab is going up every week."

Expenses were not the only things going up every week. So were Tiger's hopes and dreams. He found a Jack Nicklaus picture and decided to make a special display in his room. On the left side of a poster board, Tiger put the names of all the major golf tournaments. In a middle column, he listed how old Nicklaus was when he won the tournament listed. The final column listed Tiger's name, with empty spaces below. He planned to write in the date when *he* would win the tournament. Naturally, he planned to win each title long before the age at which Jack Nicklaus had won.

In 1985, when Tiger was nine, Earl had a heart attack. As heart attacks go, it was minor. But it still shook up the whole Woods family. Earl's doctor told him to lose some weight, watch his diet, and get more rest. It was such easy advice to hand out, but for a cyclone of energy like Earl, it was not so easy to take. Still, he promised to slow down. After all, he had to stick around to see his son paying the bills.

In 1988 Earl Woods retired from McDonnell Douglas. He now was free to travel with Tiger to tournaments. They might not have the money to fly first class or to stay in the best hotels, but they had something better. They had a bond—a deep, caring friendship—that gave each other strength. Their bond was an important boost for a twelve-year-old golfer, confident enough on a golf course but—as a soon-to-be teenager—unsure of himself in many ways. It was an equally important boost for a recently retired fifty-six-year-old man nursing a damaged heart. Individually, each was a strong and determined person. Together, they were a powerful partnership, ready to take on anything the world threw at them.

About this time, another golf pro, John Anselmo of Meadowlark Golf Course in Huntington Beach, California, joined the Woods team. He helped Tiger perfect his shots, showing him how to lift and lower them or send them to one side or another with perfect control. He taught Tiger how to put backspin on his ball and how to take it off.

A retired Navy captain, Jay Brunza, also helped Tiger. In joining the Tiger team, he focused on the young golfer's mind, helping the boy control his temper and frustrations. Relaxation did not come easy to Tiger, and Brunza found ways to let him cast away his tensions. The sports psychologist even used hypnotism to help Tiger keep his thoughts open and free.

Like the trophies, the Tiger's press coverage grew steadily. By the time he was thirteen he had won five Junior World Golf Championships and more than one hundred area tournaments. Between his golfing and his schoolwork, the boy had little time for looking at his photos and articles. Other people did. One such individual was Wally Goodwin, the golf coach at Stanford University in Palo Alto, California. Although seldom interested in players as young as Tiger, Goodwin wrote him a letter. "If you ever want to take a shot at Stanford, drop me a line," the golf coach offered.

Tiger did exactly that. In a letter dated April 23, 1989, Tiger wrote:

Dear Coach Goodwin:

Thank you for your recent letter expressing Stanford's interest in me as a future student and golfer. At first it was hard for me to understand why a university like Stanford was interested in a thirteen-year-old seventh-grader, and after talking with my father, I have come to understand and appreciate the honor you have given me. I further appreciate Mr. Sargent's interest in my future development by recommending me to you [Mr. Sargent was a university representative who saw Tiger play].

I became interested in Stanford's academics while watching the Olympics and Debbie Thomas. My goal is to obtain a quality business education. Your guidelines will be most helpful in preparing me for college life. My GPA this year is 3.86, and I plan to keep it there or higher when I enter high school.

I am working on an exercise program to increase my strength. By April, my NCGA handicap is one, and I plan to play in SCGA and maybe some AJGA tournaments this summer. My goal is to win the Junior World in July for the fourth time and to become the first player to win each age bracket. Ultimately, I would like to be a PGA professional. Next February I plan to go to Thailand and play in the Thai Open as an amateur.

I've heard a lot about your golf course and I would like to play it with my dad sometime in the future.

Hope to hear from you again.

Sincerely,

Tiger Woods

It was not the typical seventh-grade letter. In fact, it was not a typical letter in any sense. Wally Goodwin put the letter aside for the moment, but he knew it would come in handy. It might open the eyes of a few members of the Stanford golf team.

Playing in the 1990 Insurance Youth Golf Classic National was another big thrill for Tiger. Nicknamed "The Big I," the tournament allowed amateurs to play against professionals. The event always brought the best of the nation's golfers together for tense, top-flight golf. If spectators were expecting the junior-high kid from Cypress to wilt under the pressure, they must have been disappointed. Tiger, showing no signs of nervousness, trounced eight of the professionals competing in "The Big I" and gave famed PGA player John Daly a run for his money. The veteran golfer Daly managed to sneak past the young newcomer by only two strokes.

Daly and Tiger did not take the top spots at the tournament, but Tiger knew he had shot well. But he was never completely satisfied unless he came out on top. Winning was the goal, after all, and less than that was losing. Still, he was thankful for a strong performance.

"The Big I" competition also gave Tiger a chance to study the professional golfers close up. He'd been giving more and more thought to his own future, whether or not he wanted to make golf a career. Oh, he had tried other sports. On the baseball diamond, he was a natural switch-hitter. The 118 pounds that stretched over his slender five-foot, eleven-inch frame became a galloping gazelle on the football field, able to snag passes anywhere near him. That same blazing speed made him a superswift 400-meter runner on the track. But it was golf that offered him the true challenge of body and mind. Driving or chipping or putting that little ball towards that hole—there was nothing else like it. It was the U.S. Junior Amateur Championship in July of 1991 that steered Tiger closer to the decision of someday becoming a pro golfer.

The U.S. Junior Amateur Championship attracted many of the best non-pros in the country. For years Tiger had hoped to capture the title. Now, at fifteen, he felt confident he could win it. The warm breezes surrounding Tiger on the Orlando golf course seemed to whisper his name. He sailed through the early rounds, leaving other golfers in the shadows. Yes, Tiger felt home free.

It is impossible to measure the danger of overconfidence in any golfer. Playing to win by using every mental and physical tool within one's command is the secret of top golfers. However, even the very best golfer occasionally falls victim to overconfidence. It is likely the attitude that surrounded Tiger at the U.S. Junior Amateur Championship in July 1991. He was the man to beat—and Brad Zwetschke was determined to do just that.

In the final round of the tournament, Brad made no secret of his desire to win the title—and he wanted to beat Tiger. After all, Tiger entered the Junior Amateur competition with a lengthy string of championships. He was being hailed as the next Jack Nicklaus. To beat Tiger was every amateur golfer's dream.

Scores bounced back and forth in the opening rounds of play. But by the final round, Tiger was three strokes behind. If he really wanted to win, he knew it would take his full concentrated effort. Tiger gave it just that, carefully analyzing each shot and executing every stroke with perfect poise and precision. On the 18th hole he managed to tie Brad, leading to a playoff round. Whoever could score the lowest on the next hole would be the tournament winner.

Ordinarily, the Orlando air was fresh, but at this point the tension seemed to make the atmosphere thick. Brad led off on the final hole. The pressure was on, and he showed it. By the time he sank his ball in the cup, Brad was two strokes over par for a double bogey. Tiger knew what he had to do to win. The nervousness seemed to slip off Brad and climb inside Tiger. His shots were measured and direct but not even close to many of his past performances. However, he managed to tip his final putt in with one stroke over par for a bogey. He was the winner!

Winning the U.S. Junior Amateur Championship gave Tiger much more than another trophy: He learned a lesson about being too overconfident. At fifteen, he was picking up many valuable lessons. They would come in handy in the years ahead.

Chapter Five
Staying on Course

The date was February 27, 1992.

Tiger was preparing to tee off at the Riviera Country Club in Los Angeles, California. He was playing at the Nissan Open, a Professional Golfers Association event. Only sixteen, he was making history. He was the youngest person in PGA history ever invited to play in a professional tournament. His past performances in golf competition had earned him the invitation.

Tiger's participation in the Nissan Open also was special for another reason. It was a school day, and he was skipping! True, school officials at Western High School in Anaheim, California, were aware of and had approved his absence. Still, for honors sophomore Tiger Woods, it felt strange setting his ball on a tee while his classmates were struggling with gerunds and infinitives in a classroom.

Tiger's appearance at the Nissan Open also had a dark side. The tournament chairman had received three phone calls threatening Tiger's life. Someone did not like the young golfer being given a special exemption to take part in the tournament. The caller threatened to kill Tiger. Three special security guards were assigned to mingle with the crowd, making sure that no harm came to Tiger. "Only sixteen years old," he joked, "and I've already had my first death threat."

Tiger hoped to perform well before the crowd. After all, the tournament was close to his hometown, and many of the spectators were his friends and supporters. The high-school golf team had come to cheer on their colleague. Of course, Earl and Tida were there too.

But Tiger was not use to the chatter and noise as he played. The television cameras bothered him. He could hear the commentators' remarks. It was just like his father had warned him: not every situation would allow for perfect concentration on the game, and this tourna-ment was one of those situations. Whether from the action of the game or the stress of the surroundings, Tiger pulled a back muscle. He sent tee shots flying, not with his usual precision but to the sides. Clip shots failed, and putts rolled too short or too long. By the time his tryouts ended, Tiger was six strokes short of making the cut.

As disappointed as Tiger was, he looked at the Nissan Open as a learning experience. "I learned I'm not that good," he admitted. "I've got a lot of growing to do."

The summer of 1992 offered Tiger the chance to do some growing. When he headed to Wollaston Golf Club in Massachusetts, he had one goal in mind: to defend his U.S. Junior Championship title. In the forty-five years since the tournament began, no player had ever managed to repeat a victory performance. Tiger liked making history.

The sixteen-year-old golfer spent a lot of time examining his weaknesses. A major problem was his ability to control the distance of his shots, especially when teeing off. Using the same positioning and the same swing with the same club, Tiger could send the ball hurling 150, 165, or 180 yards. He knew he took too many risk shots. It was fine to be creative at times, and often Tiger's unique shots paid off. However, there were times when he took unnecessary chances that left him in awkward spots on a course.

Tiger liked the course at Wollaston. The greens were beautifully trimmed, the trees stood like tall handsome sentinels against the skyline, and the air tasted clean and fresh.

One by one, Tiger cast off his opponents. Although his game was not fantastic, it was strong enough to blast away the competition. By the time Sunday arrived, the day of the championship battle, Tiger was pitted against Mark Wilson of Menomonee Falls, Wisconsin.

People started arriving early for the final round, some driving up to 150 miles to witness the Woods-Wilson clash. The U.S. Amateur event usually attracted a few hundred spectators, but with Tiger's reputation was growing, more than one thousand people showed up.

Mark got off to an early lead, causing a few spectators to lift their eyebrows in wonder. But as play progressed, Tiger picked up his game, cutting into his opponent's score with each hole. With six holes left, Tiger was two strokes behind.

Mark could not maintain the pace. Tiger seemed to reach into his golf bag and pull out not only the right club but also just the right amount of determination. In two of the last three holes, Tiger slipped ahead and snagged his second U.S. Junior Championship. Earl was the first person on the 18th hole to embrace his son.

That championship was the high of the summer for Tiger. Winning a championship was always special, but Tiger found he particularly enjoyed the special feeling that came with making golf history.

No matter how well Tiger played during the summer, he was always eager to return to school in the fall. He was proud of being a member of both the golf and the track teams at Western High at Anaheim, California. Although he might attract a lot of attention on a golf course, at Western he was just one of the Pioneers, the nickname given to the student body.

Tiger loved hanging out with his friends. He spent hours playing video games, biking, and catching the latest movie at a local mall. Sometimes he pleased his father by listening to jazz music, but most of the time he liked rap and rhythm and blues.

A high-school growth spurt tacked on six inches in two years, and Tiger tried desperately to put more meat on his bones. He gobbled down burgers and chomped away on tacos from fast-food restaurants. Pizza was another food favorite, accompanied by a strawberry milkshake. Yet while his body stretched to six feet, eleven inches tall, his weight stayed steady at 140 pounds.

His slender frame slid comfortably behind the wheel of the blue Toyota Supra, a gift from his father, when Tiger got his driver's license.

Tiger and his father were constant companions at tournaments. "Thanks to him being there, I seldom got homesick," Tiger recalled. But the relationship was not without an occasional bump.

One nasty confrontation took place at the Orange Bowl International Junior Invitational on December 30, 1992, during the final round of play. Word spread around the crowd that it was Tiger's seventeenth birthday, and the people wanted to share their good wishes.

"Happy birthday to you . . . happy birthday to you . . ."

The merry sounds of the spectators drifted across the Biltmore Golf Course at Coral Gables, Florida. Tiger flashed his bright smile and waved his cap to the audience. He had learned to appreciate the gallery of people who followed him. Life was good, his game was good, and the fans were good. "I'd like to be the Michael Jordan of golf," he told reporters in a moment when his spirits were soaring. Few individuals doubted the probability of that happening.

But Earl was worried. He always worried. Whatever happened, he wanted his son to stay focused on his game. Distractions could be dangerous. As he heard the crowd singing "Happy Birthday" and watched his son's reactions, Earl knew Tiger would have a hard time staying focused on his golf game.

Earl was right. From the moment he teed off, Tiger played sloppily. His shots were off target, and his pacing was erratic. After missing an easy putt, Tiger showed an unusual side to his playing style—he pouted. From the sidelines, Earl fumed. Parents are not allowed to speak to their children during competition, so he bristled within. By the end of the match Tiger was trailing the winner by three strokes, and he had to win a playoff round to capture second place.

Birthday or not, Earl railed into his son as the bus took the two of them back to the hotel. "Who do you think you are?" Earl demanded. "Golf owes you nothing. You were a quitter out there on that golf course. You never quit! You understand me? You never quit!"

The words struck like hard-hit golf balls. Tiger could not find words to answer. Even if he could have found the words, he was too afraid to speak. From that day on, he promised that he would never quit, no matter how many strokes he was behind. He would give every shot his best!

Chapter Six
Making Big Decisions

In the final months of 1992, Tiger Woods was named the top amateur golfer in the country by *Golf Digest, Golf Week,* and *Golf World.* He was hitting the ball at 122 miles an hour, and his drives were sailing well over 300 yards. Polishing his accumulated trophies was a full day's work, and listing his tournament victories took up a full column of newspaper copy.

Although it was Tiger's golf accomplishments that brought sports writers to his doorstep, the teenager talked about much more than sports. He clearly had opinions, and he was willing to share them openly.

"A kid growing up with parents who love him has many advantages. My parents always let me talk, let me help make decisions, gave me freedoms," Tiger explained. "They let me know if I made a mistake, but they were reasonable about their punishments. There was nothing I couldn't share with them. They were always willing to listen."

Tiger also spoke openly about being a minority. "Actually, if one looks at it mathematically, I'm Asian. Yet in the United States, people label me as black. If you have one drop of black blood in you in this country, you are considered black. And how important it is for this country to talk about the subject?"

Tiger's thoughts showed not only that he knew how to handle a golf club but that he could think and express himself clearly. There was much more to him than what people saw on the golf course. "Sometimes, Tiger seemed like Superman," observed one of his classmates. "He had it all: good grades, good-looking girlfriend, good family, great talent in sports, lots of friends . . ."

Nevertheless, in the spring of 1993 Tiger showed he was definitely human. His glands swelled, his throat felt dry and scratchy, and he couldn't shake off a high fever. His body seemed to wear out easily. For the first time in his life, he did not feel like playing golf. The diagnosis was mononucleosis.

For three weeks Tiger did not lift a golf club. But when the Junior Amateur Tournament came around, he was ready. No one had ever won the title three times. Tiger hoped to write some new history.

The tournament was taking place in the northwest part of the country, at the Waverly Country Club in Portland, Oregon. The June breezes danced across the course, and Tiger breathed the fresh air in deeply. He was not fully recovered, but he was ready to play. He asked Jay Brunza to be his caddy. Tiger was sure Jay would help provide the psychological upswing that he might need.

The early tournament rounds slipped by quickly with no major surprises. The final round pitted Tiger against another high-school standout, Ryan Armour. Almost five thousand spectators flocked to Waverly to witness the competition between two junior masters of the game.

Ryan took an early lead in the contest, displaying both strength and careful maneuvering. It was obvious he hoped to prevent Tiger from getting his trio of victories at the tournament. As they approached the 17th hole, Tiger trailed by two strokes. Every shot counted.

On the 17th hole, Ryan parred. The pressure was on Tiger to sink a putt eight feet from the cup. It would give him a birdie, one under par for the hole. Could he do it?

Tiger consulted with Jay, out of earshot of the crowd. When he took his position, one thought raced through Tiger's head: "Got to be like Nicklaus. Got to will this in the cup." Tiger assumed his stance, with his feet apart and his putter poised. He hit the ball and watched it roll perfectly into the cup. Yes! A birdie. Now he was only down by one.

When Tiger teed off on the final hole, the ball sailed more than three hundred yards but came to rest in a rough to the side of the fairway. Using a three iron, he lifted his ball high in the air, but to no avail: It landed in a sand trap, some forty feet from the green. Some spectators shook their heads. Even Earl looked down. This jam would be tough for Tiger to escape.

Tiger gritted his teeth, drawing from within all his mental and physical power. He slowly and carefully planned his shot, swung his club, and connected. The crowd watched as the ball arched high and then dropped, rolling ten feet from the hole.

Once again many within the crowd shook their heads. That ten feet looked like a long distance to many. Tiger approached the ball, practiced a couple of swings, and tapped the sphere forward. It rolled straight ahead and dropped into the cup. Tiger smiled as the crowd roared its approval. He'd tied the match.

In the playoff for the championship, Tiger regained confidence. His tee shot put the ball only twenty feet from the cup. Another shot cut sixteen feet off that distance, and a final putt gave him a three-stroke total. Ryan gave it his best effort, but he took four shots to sink the ball. Tiger had come back from his illness to win the Junior Am for an unprecedented third time. Earl raced onto the green and hugged his son. "I'm so proud of you," the older man said. Those words meant a lot to Tiger.

"It was the most amazing comeback of my entire career," Tiger told reporters. "I had to play the best two holes of my life . . . and I did it."

Tiger's joy was short-lived. When he headed to Houston

to take part in the U.S. Amateur at Champions Golf Club, he carried impressive baggage. Having won the Junior Amateur title three times, he now had a chance to become the first golfer to win the Junior Am and the U.S. Am in the same year.

Tiger started off with shooting well, staying at par with occasional birdies and an eagle. However, as the match progressed, Tiger showed trouble with his swing. On the 17th hole of the final round, he hit his ball into a side bunker. His chief opponent, Paul Page, was up by two strokes but now was caught in a sand trap. A thunderstorm suddenly passed over the area, and tournament officials stopped the action for five hours until it passed. When play resumed, sand covered Page's ball. An official ordered the area raked and Page's ball returned to its original lie. It was a major break for Page, and he went on to win the tournament. "I didn't expect to lose on a rake drop like that," Tiger said. Paul Page was thrilled with the win, but he would be the last player to defeat Tiger in United States Golf Association competition. In the years ahead, Tiger would run his USGA match record to 42-3, winning all eighteen of his next eighteen matches and three U.S. Amateur titles.

Chapter Seven

Growing Pains

Tiger knew it wasn't just a thunderstorm that caused him to lose the U.S. Amateur: his own shots, especially his drives, were to blame. He was hitting the ball with plenty of speed, but his hip movement was off, causing a loose swing. If anyone could help with the problem, it was Butch Harmon. Butch was the son of Claude Harmon, who had won the Masters back in 1948. Much like Tiger, Butch Harmon had been weaned on a golf club. He had worked with golf notables Greg Norman, Davis Love III, and Steve Elkington.

Once Earl put Tiger and Butch together, the pair clicked. Butch videotaped Tiger hitting shots. Then the two carefully analyzed every movement, every precise second of positioning and poise. Butch suggested a wider stance, a wider arc at the top of his backswing, and less hip turn. Tiger followed Butch's suggestions. Sure enough, his swing improved.

In the year that followed, Tiger and Butch had little time to get together. Tiger was finishing up his high-school career, while Butch had duties at his country club. But they sent videos back and forth through the mail, and the telephone wires buzzed with their constant help sessions.

"Tiger Woods was good, real good," Butch admitted. "I'd like to think I made him a little bit better. But he was awful darn good to begin with."

Chapter Eight
Taking New Steps

Tiger Woods entered his final year at Western High School in Anaheim with the same expectations as other seniors: This was the *big* year, the last one for homecoming, plays, and proms. It was a time to remember the past, enjoy the present, and plan for the future.

Stanford University had loomed tall in Tiger's mind for a long time. He knew he wanted to become a professional golfer someday, and he certainly wanted to play in college. Stanford boasted not only a fine golf team but also a top-quality academic program. Would it be possible to maintain high grades while playing college golf and keeping an active tournament career going besides? Maybe the University of Nevada at Las Vegas or Arizona State would be better choices. Each school had a solid academic reputation and a decent golf program, too. Yet they seemed to score extra points in the social column: lots of parties and fun in a more relaxed atmosphere.

The decision was no easy one. Arizona State gradually slipped out of the running. It boiled down to Stanford or UNLV. Tiger weighed each one again and again. Stanford carried a worldwide reputation for its business program. Companies lined up to hire Stanford business graduates. But that gorgeous climate at Las Vegas! People said it never rained there, especially *never* on golf courses. Tiger

agonized so much over which school to attend that he became physically ill.

Finally, Tiger made his decision. The announcement that Tiger had picked Stanford was made in the Western High gym on November 10, 1993. Tiger's love for the school dated back years. He probably wouldn't be able to focus as much on his golf game as he'd like because of his academic requirements, yet he had to look at the long-range picture. Just like on the golf course, it was important to look at the whole picture, not just one shot at a time. He was used to bunkers on the fairway, and just as they impeded his golf shots, the demands of Stanford's scholastic standards would challenge him as well. But he promised to give it his best, and Earl and Tida supported his decision.

No one was happier with Tiger's decision than Wally Goodwin, Stanford's golf coach. Ever since he received the seventh-grader's letter, he had followed Tiger's career with much interest. "When you're lucky enough to sign the best junior player who's ever lived, you have a star in your midst," Goodwin said. But the sage coach knew his team would not be stepping aside for any freshman. The newcomer would have to win his spot on the team just like he'd won countless tournaments and trophies. "They're going to beat him like a drum for a while," Goodwin laughed.

And they did. Notah Begay, Steve Burdick, Brad Lanning, Casey Martin, and William Yanagisawa were not about to bow before an incoming freshman no matter how his impressive credentials were. They were ready to challenge him, test him, even beat him on the course. After all, a freshman was a lowly freshman. He had to earn his place.

Tiger wanted it no other way. But there was one tournament trophy Tiger was determined to capture before entering college: the United States Amateur Championship. Competing against all ages, the victor claimed the title as the best amateur golfer in the country.

If Tiger could do it, he'd be the first golfer to win both the Junior Amateur *and* the U.S. Amateur as well as become the youngest winner in the history of the Amateur tournament. Tiger loved those superlative titles and the thought of reaching new milestones in the world of golf.

Golf fans crowded the Tournament Players Club-Sawgrass Stadium in Ponte Vedra Beach, Florida, for the Amateur opening day Thursday, August 25, 1994. It was good weather for golf, with soft breezes fanning the course. Tiger had little trouble against the early challengers, and Sunday found him facing Trip Kuehne for the championship. However, the weather had turned humid and hot, with mosquitoes and dragonflies dive-bombing the course. Tiger usually wore a baseball cap, but on this day he showed up in a straw hat with black band.

The winner of the Amateur was the golfer who posted the lower score after two rounds (thirty-six holes) of golf in the final pairing. Tiger knew beating Trip would take a major effort. Jay Brunza was called in to caddy and to keep Tiger psyched up. Despite Jay's coaching and Earl's moral support, Tiger floundered in the opening holes. He was six strokes down after thirteen holes, further down that anyone who had ever before won the Amateur Tournament.

During the lunch break Tiger showered and changed clothes. He hoped to wash away his shaky beginning and start the afternoon fresh. Before he teed off, Earl whispered into his son's ear. "Let the legend grow," he said, and Tiger knew what his father meant. It was time, time to put on the steam.

Total concentration. Poise and precision. Ignore the people. Focus on the ball and the cup. Tiger put everything he knew into his game. Gradually, he picked up strokes on Trip. Five. Four. After twenty-seven of the required thirty-six holes, Tiger was only three strokes behind.

All Tiger could think about was the ball and the cup, the ball and the cup. His confidence level soared. He knocked off another stroke. Then another. On the 16th hole, he birdied, tying Trip.

On the 17th hole, Tiger took a big chance. It was a short hole-only 139 yards. But the hole was as dangerous as it was short. The green was surrounded by water. If Tiger hit a bad shot and ended up in the water, he would be penalized a stroke—and he couldn't afford that kind of penalty.

Although Tiger was known for his creativity on the course, no one expected him to try a pitching wedge to tee off with. But Tiger knew how to judge the wind. If he could hit the ball high and make it drop, he'd clear the water and land on the green. Another stroke and he'd be in the hole.

All eyes were on Tiger as he approached the tee. He took his time, appraising the entire situation. Focus. No distractions. With his usual smooth form and determined poise, he brought the club down behind the ball. The ball soared high, and the spectators gasped. Moments later the ball landed, took a hop on the green, then spun back and landed a scant three feet away from the edge.

People applauded, impressed with the eighteen-year-old's daring and talent. But Tiger knew he wasn't done yet. If he was to score a birdie, and that's what he needed, he had to land a fourteen-foot putt.

Once on the green, Tiger surveyed the situation carefully. The wind. The tilt of the land. The lie of his ball. Finally, he eased into position and hit the ball. It headed directly toward the cup and dropped in. Birdie!

With the crowd applauding, Tiger pumped his right arm jubilantly into the air. He was in the lead now. He felt sure he could keep it. And he did just that.

Trip Kuehne was not only a great opponent—he was a fine loser as well. "Super job!" he told Tiger, adding a high five and firm hug. "You deserved to win."

Tiger matched Trip's sportsmanship when he spoke with reporters later. "It's an amazing feeling to come from that many down to beat a great player," he said.

More and more people wondered if Tiger was going to turn pro. It seemed like a natural time. After all, he was playing great golf. He could go to college anytime. Stanford University would be around in ten or twenty more years.

But in the fall of 1994, Tiger Woods packed his bags. The college classroom was calling.

Chapter Nine
Staying Focused

"Hey, Urkel! Carry my golfbag!"

Tiger grimaced. It was no easy task being the only freshman on the Stanford golf team. The senior members of the squad had no intention of doing the freshman from Cypress any special favors. The upperclassmen teased Tiger when he wore glasses instead of the usual contacts he'd acquired in high school. Urkel was the nerdy kid on the TV show *Family Matters,* and Tiger's teammates taunted him with the nickname. When the team traveled, Tiger drew the worst hotel room and had to help load the suitcases and equipment.

Between classes, homework, and golf, there was little time for anything else. Tiger relaxed by biking fifty or sixty miles along the California coast. He liked to party when time allowed. But even at social occasions he was teased. "He looks smooth when he's golfing," one of his friends observed. "But he dances like an octopus."

Tiger could take the good-natured kidding from his classmates and friends. After all, he was a freshman, at the bottom of the ladder.

But Tiger had a hard time dealing with abrasive reporters who tracked him down on the Stanford campus and demanded interviews. "Do you know when you're going to turn pro?" was a constant question. "You're not

going to stay here for four years, are you? Why not go out and make the big bucks while you can?"

There were ugly phone calls, too—and nasty letters. "Give it up, black boy, you ain't no good." Why would strangers want to write such trash? And memories of that first day of kindergarten so many years ago came back to haunt him.

Shortly before Christmas break, Tiger walked across the Stanford campus one night. Suddenly, he felt an arm wrapped around his chest. "Tiger, give me your wallet," a voice in the darkness ordered. The stranger whirled Tiger around, butted him in the mouth with a knife handle, and grabbed his watch and a gold chain Tida had given him. The man quickly disappeared. Although Tiger was not seriously hurt, he felt badly. The man had called him by name. The experience left Tiger shaken and saddened.

Being named *Golf World's* Man of the Year boosted Tiger's spirits. So did winning Player of the Year honors from the *Los Angeles Times* newspaper. The coming year, 1995, promised more opportunities. As the winner of the U.S. Amateur Tournament, Tiger was eligible to compete in the Masters, the U.S. Open, and the British Open. Not bad for a college freshman! But it meant juggling his college schedule with high-powered golfing competition.

The Masters, held in Augusta, Georgia, conflicted head-on with Stanford's final exams in the spring. Legend had it the greens at Augusta were smooth and slick. Tiger practiced on the university gym floors. They were closer to the Augusta greens than the golf courses around Stanford.

Studying for tests and practicing for the Masters took its toll on Tiger. He lost his appetite and couldn't sleep. He wanted to get good grades, *and* he wanted to do well in Augusta.

Actually, it had only been five years that black people had played at the Masters. The founder of the tournament wanted only white people to compete. Oh, there was a place for black people at the prestigious tournament—they could be caddies and carry the clubs for white participants.

But Tiger Woods was no caddie, that was certain. His golf bag was black leather with "United States" spelled out in gold letters. When rain started to fall during the first round of play, he pulled out a bright red, white, and blue umbrella.

There would be no victory dance at this first Masters tournament, and no green sportscoat either. Tiger's drives were long, sailing straight and true with powerful speed. But his clip shots and approach shots were off. Tiger returned to Stanford just in time to take another final exam. He also learned that the National Collegiate Athletic Association (NCAA) was displeased that he had used golf clubs that pro Gregg Norman had recommended while competing at the Masters. The NCAA thought Tiger should have used golf clubs used by the Stanford golf team because Tiger was an active member of the squad. He was given a brief suspension.

However, the trip to Augusta had changed Tiger, and he knew it. He wrote to the Augusta golf officials, thanking them for "the most wonderful week of my life. It is here that I left my youth behind," wrote Tiger, "and became a man."

But that "man" was not the old Tiger. More and more people were watching his every move, and he was showing the strain from the scrutiny. Whenever he played in a PGA event or college tournament, people wanted to know when he was going to turn pro. Reporters often called on the telephone, interrupting his studies. Tiger tried to be polite. That quality had always been a part of his game. Tida had instilled the importance of sportsmanship when Tiger was just getting started. But now Tiger was kicking his golf bag and throwing his clubs.

But Tiger's problems were not only mental: His body was causing him problems, too. A knee required surgery, and his right shoulder was causing him deep pain. He struggled to keep his weight up; his 150 pounds gave him a scarecrow likeness over his 6'2" frame. His usual bouncy stride slowed, and his eyes glazed a bit.

Matters came to a head in June of 1995. While playing in the U.S. Open, Tiger swung hard to get his ball out of the rough on the Shinnecock Hills. He grimaced in pain, clutching his wrist. It was sprained, and Tiger had to drop out of the tournament.

It was time to look things over, time to examine the situation. Tiger was nineteen years old, but he was pushing himself like he had only a couple years of golf ahead of him. Not only that, his grades were not where they could be. He was an "A" student in high school, but he was struggling for Bs in some college classes. Part of that struggle was due to the pressure he put on himself. It was time to ease up and take time to enjoy life a little bit more.

When Tiger arrived at St. Andrews in Scotland to play in the British Open, he appeared more relaxed. The sprained wrist had mended well, and Tiger hit well, even against powerful winds. No one really expected him to win, and he lived up to those expectations. But he felt good about playing again, and he was eager to defend his title at the U.S. Amateur Tournament at Newport, Rhode Island.

Tiger was greeted by a giant collection of fans. TIGER ROARS! one banner declared, carried by a group of youngsters. *They* were the ones roaring whenever their hero looked in their direction and flashed that wide smile.

From the very first tee shot, Tiger took his time. A hearty wind danced across the Rhode Island course, and the defending champion took every opportunity to gauge its force and direction. He calculated every movement, driving, chipping, and putting with care and certainty. Even when he slipped behind, he played with unbelievable calm.

Playing a total of 36 holes, Tiger slipped ahead on the

24th. It was a nip-and-tuck battle, with challengers at his heels every step of the course. On the final hole, Tiger led by one stroke. He teed off, sending the ball 265 yards. Using an eight iron, he snapped the ball 140 yards away to the green, and the ball ended up a foot and a half from the cup. Slowly, meticulously, Tiger measured the shot from every angle. Then he rose and tapped the ball in.

The crowd exploded in cheers as Tiger and his father hugged. Few people could claim back-to-back victories in tournaments, yet Tiger Woods had now won the U.S. Amateur championships two years in a row!

But for Tiger, it was more than a double win for the record books. He was convinced that his game was now intact. That last hole had convinced him. That special second shot between his tee shot and the final putt gave him a real push forward. "I didn't have that shot last year and I didn't have it at the Masters," he said. But he had it now, and that meant a lot to his confidence level.

Chapter Ten
Making Golf History

When he returned to Stanford to begin his sophomore year in the fall of 1995, Tiger was glad to see his old friends. Despite their frequent teasing, his teammates from the golf team had learned to respect the guy with the smooth swing and the lowest score. Tiger always seemed to keep his cool and maintain his edge in competition. He was consistent, leading the team to one victory after another. Yet he displayed neither arrogance nor boasting. At each match, Tiger rolled into action, did his job superbly, then packed up to begin "psyching up" for the next opponent. In conference action, the Stanford Cardinals were the team to beat.

Not only did Tiger enjoy his position on the golf team, but he loved the stimulating classroom discussions, the coursework, the lectures. "The place is full of geniuses!" he told his parents. He knew that if he kept up with his work, he could hold his own whether it be in a student-to-professor dialogue or on any test or project. Tiger was not short on brainpower, but he never saw himself among the "geniuses" on campus

Tiger liked playing by the rules, both in the classroom and out of it. Cheating was not for him; he liked to get his grades honestly. But sometimes those NCAA rules seemed ridiculous. No other player on the Stanford golf team

played in professional competitions, but Tiger's win at the U.S. Amateur allowed him that privilege. It was an honor—but it was a nuisance, too. First, there was that suspension after the Masters competition. On another occasion, he had supper with professional golfer Arnold Palmer, who paid the bill. It was purely a social affair, but when it got back to NCAA officials, they reprimanded Tiger. An amateur college athlete had no business talking his sport over with a pro and letting that pro pay for the privilege. To Tiger, Arnold Palmer was not just a pro golfer—he was a personal friend. Somehow it seemed like someone from the NCAA was looking over his shoulder, watching his every move. It was an uneasy feeling. Tiger maintained his cool, but his father found it more difficult. "Wish those NCAA folks would leave the boy alone," he grumbled.

But on the golf course Tiger enjoyed good feeling among his teammates. As a sophomore, he enjoyed more respect—especially since he led the group against every opponent. He not only constantly worked on his own game, but he also was willing to help his peers. He patiently helped his buddies, demonstrating his own techniques and showing what he had seen professional golfers do. Many of his teammates improved their game, and the Stanford record improved too.

The reporters continued to dog Tiger with questions about him turning pro. Clearly, it was not a matter of if he was going to. The big question was *when*. Tiger worked out a lot during the winter of 1995-96, adding muscle to his arms and legs. His weight climbed a few pounds to 155, and he felt strong and in shape.

Returning to the Masters in the spring of 1996 by virtue of his 1995 U.S. Amateur victory, Tiger had a hard time focusing on his game. Once more he was badgered by reporters demanding to know when he was turning pro. "I'd like to focus on my game here," Tiger said. "I'm really not sure what I plan to do in the future, but I'm sure I'd like to play well here in Augusta." The media crowd understood—momentarily— and then again wanted to know when Tiger was going to turn professional. With his concentration flagging, Tiger did not even manage to make the cut at the Master's. On the greens, his putts were off. Most people attributed his shooting to youthful impatience, but those closer to Tiger knew that he had been distracted by a preoccupation with his future.

But Tiger's blazing golf play returned back at Stanford. In post-season play, the Cardinal crew captured the Pac-10 Championship and went on to win the Western Regional Championship. Tiger consistently posted scores in the 60s, motivating his teammates and devastating his opponents.

In June, Tiger headed to the NCAA Tournament in Chattanooga, Tennessee. Of the record-number fifteen thousand people who attended, many had come to see Tiger. "Go, T!" someone would yell, and the shout became a chant. "The Tiger is da Man!" another would holler. That, too, became a refrain. It took fifteen guards to handle the gallery of fans following him on the final round.

Tiger did not disappoint the people. His drive shots hurled 380 yards, and his chips out of bunkers seemed drawn to the cup. If a miracle putt was called for, Tiger delivered, and the crowd would erupt into a giant cheer as the ball danced around in the cup.

Just as the fans appreciated Tiger, he appreciated them right back. He paused to sign autographs, slap high fives, and throw golf balls to those fans begging for them. The smile was constant, his thank-yous never stopped. He didn't play his best golf, but he played well enough to snag the NCAA championship by four strokes under his closest competitor.

As soon as he finished at Chattanooga, Tiger zipped back to Stanford. He had to finish up a major accounting term paper and take a final exam in African literature. It was an exhausting schedule, one few college student could maintain. "You got to want it bad," one sports columnist wrote, "to jump through the hoops Tiger Woods jumps through."

Then Tiger was off to Detroit to play in the U.S. Open. He was a spinning top, whirling around from golf course to classroom, trying to maintain his direction and stamina. At the Open, he started off fine and then fizzled in the final holes. His putts were long, short, everything but in the cup. There were no Tiger smiles, no happy waves. Angry at his performance, he tossed his equipment in his car and zoomed out of the parking lot.

By July, Tiger had calmed down. He arrived to play in the British Open again smiling and hoping for a solid performance. Despite the wind, Tiger shot strong, well-calculated shots. He mustered up the power when needed, then eased into soft nimble shots on the greens. His body control was perfect, his swing natural. "I feel good," he declared, "like I've found a whole new style of playing. I'm playing within myself, and the game seems easier." Tiger ended up tying the Open record for the lowest score as an amateur — a sparkling 271.

Then he returned to the States, to the Pumpkin Ridge Golf Club in Cornelius, Oregon. Tiger was shooting for his third consecutive U.S. Amateur title.

There was the usual excitement surrounding the tournament, but there was an extra bit of chatter among the fans in attendance. Spotted in the gallery was Philip Knight, kingpin at Nike Corporation, the giant sportswear conglomerate. "Hey, just came down to watch some golf," the businessman told reporters. True, the Nike international headquarters was located in nearby Beaverton, some fifteen miles away. But anyone who truly believed Knight's explanation for his appearance had to be very naive. Most knew Tiger was a hot prospect for Nike. The company was always looking for top athletes to endorse their products—stars such as basketball's Michael Jordan and tennis's Pete Sampras. Of course, Tiger was ineligible for such a role, at least, while he was attending Stanford and playing as an amateur.

If Tiger's mind was on Nike, endorsements, or turning pro, it didn't show in his performance at the U.S. Amateur tournament. As usual, it was one step at a time—and this step was to capture one more championship. He shot six super rounds to qualify for the final thirty-six holes.

On the final day of play, Tiger tried to appear relaxed and casual. He wore a red polo shirt, red being his victory color, and traded light banter with his caddie, Bryon Bell, a good friend from high school days. His black cap displayed the words U.S. Amateur and an American flag. He nodded to the gallery, but his attention was focused on the ball and the course. His opponent was Steve Scott, a top student golfer from the University of Florida.

As he'd done so often, Tiger started slow. Scott crept into a lead, never by more than a couple of strokes, but in tournament finals a lead like that is tough to overcome. As the two players approached the 34th hole, Scott led by two strokes. It would take Tiger's best playing to beat his opponent.

And that's just what Tiger delivered. He managed to birdie the 34th hole. With that birdie, he cut Scott's lead to one stroke. Now, if he could just do it again.

Tiger's tee shot on the 35th hole was all right, but the approach shot left him thirty-five feet from the hole. He was obviously disgusted with himself, and the crowd sensed his anger. But he focused—focused like never before—and putted. The ball silently slipped over the grass toward the hole. Would it stop short? It seemed that it would, for just a moment. Then it dropped in. Tiger's face exploded in the widest smile imaginable as he thrust his right fist into the air. He'd tied the match!

The tie continued through regulation match play, and a 37th hole as well. The 38th hole was a par three. Steve Scott, obviously drained from the tension, needed four strokes. Tiger saw his chance. With a strong drive teeing off, followed by an approach that landed him eighteen inches from the hole, Tiger bore down. He tapped the ball gently. It rolled forward and in.

Three-peat! Tiger had won the U.S. Amateur Championship three times in a row. Once again, he had made golfing history. There was no doubt he was the best amateur golfer in the country. Now it was time to take another step.

Chapter Eleven
Turning Pro

August 18, 1996.

Tiger stared down at the piece of paper in his hands. The twenty-year-old read nervously to himself as he prepared to make a formal announcement. Reporters prepared to take notes while TV crews adjusted their cameras. Most of them already knew why they had been summoned to the Brown Deer Creek Golf Course in Milwaukee. It was the start of the Greater Milwaukee Open—a tournament for professional golfers—and their ranks were about to increase by one.

"I guess, 'Hello, world,'" Tiger said softly.

Hmmm. What could that mean? "Hello, world." Soon those two words became very significant. They were the logo that Nike had created to launch their new line of Tiger Woods products. What better way to start this particular presentation?

Tiger carefully read a statement announcing his decision to turn pro to the press. He thanked his parents for supporting him through his life, both on and off the golf course, and for helping him reach his decision. He thanked others who had helped him grow as a person and as an athlete. He expressed gratitude to Stanford University, to the Junior Golf Association, and to other groups who had helped him. At the end of his comments, Tiger answered questions. He told the reporters it had been an "exciting and difficult year." Juggling a schedule of academics and sports tournaments certainly had been "exciting" but it also had been exhausting. Deciding if and when to turn pro provided the "difficult" part of the year.

"Going into the Amateur, I knew that I would make a decision—after the Amateur. Should I or shouldn't? I knew that after I won, there was not much to achieve in amateur golf."

With a grin, Tiger promised his parents he *would* graduate from college one day. But he was convinced that the time was right to turn pro—a dream he'd had ever since he had watched Jack Nicklaus on TV. Perhaps, too, he could open up the game of golf to minorities just like Jackie Robinson had done with baseball in 1947.

Underprivileged kids were a special concern to Tiger. He knew youngsters in the inner city had little chance to play golf. They did not have the money or the facilities. Tiger promised to hold clinics so poor kids could get a chance to learn to play the game of golf.

Tiger's tone was modest and honest. Everything made perfect sense. Not only "sense": Tiger's decision made dollars too. It was announced Tiger had signed a $40 million dollar contract with Nike to endorse sportswear, while Titleist golf balls and clubs had lined up a deal for $20 million. Tiger was a multimillionaire even though he hadn't even teed off once as a professional golfer.

Most people who read and heard of Tiger's announcement applauded his plans. "Such a good boy," said one middle-aged mother. "It's time he made the switch," declared a Saturday golfer of retirement age.

But many pro golfers felt Tiger might be hurrying too fast. Amateur golf was one thing, but playing with the best of the best? Was he really ready for that? Could he endure the strain, the intensity?

Earl Woods minced no words in answering the naysayers. "He's ready to take anyone on," he stated in his firm military voice. "Maybe some of these guys are just a little bit scared of the new guy on the block. Time will tell, and so will talent. Tiger's got both of those on his side."

A crowd of twenty thousand people turned out for the start of the Milwaukee Open.

Something new had been added to Tiger Woods's usually stylish outfit. Eagle-eyed spectators could count sixteen Nike logos emblazoning his black shoes, cap, pants, and striped polo shirt.

With his first tee shot as a pro, Tiger blasted his ball 336 yards down the fairway. Eyebrows lifted and people were impressed. But in the rounds that followed, Tiger seemed sluggish. He was tired and it showed. On the final hole, he delighted the crowd with a hole-in-one. But it was only enough for him to tie for sixtieth place, giving him a $2,544 check. Some of the pros nodded, convinced they were right that Tiger was not ready. He didn't see it that way, because he was finally getting paid to do what he loved to do most!

In his second professional outing, Tiger picked up the pace. He played in the Bell Canadian Open in Oakville, Ontario. The northern breezes helped carry his ball well, and he carried away $37,500 in a tie for eleventh place.

The Quad City Classic in Coal Valley, Illinois, during mid-September offered Tiger a good chance to score his first pro victory. The crowd of one hundred thousand during the four days of play was an assortment people of both sexes and of all ages and colors. It was a festive atmosphere, cheerful and friendly except when golfers were shooting—and then no sounds could be heard. Kids scrambled to see Tiger, and his warm smile delighted them. Tiger held the lead into the final day of play, but then he sent two balls into the water on the 4th hole. Rallying with six birdies, he could only muster a 72 for the day's play, placing him fifth. The check for $42,150 brought him little cheer.

"I had a three-shot lead," he said, shaking his head to reporters. "I let it slip away, very quickly, in a heartbeat. I putted horribly."

Clearly, Tiger was his own worst critic.

The B.C. Open in Endicott, New York, was usually a decent tournament, attracting a variety of professional golfers and a sedate collection of onlookers. But with Tiger competing, the event turned into a spectacle. The crowd scrambled over rocks and climbed buildings to get a good look at the action "Tiger! Tiger!" was a recurring chant, and the other pro golfers begged for silence when they shot. Tiger walked away with third place, boosting his winnings to more than $140,000 in four tournaments. It was enough for Tiger to buy a house in Orlando, Florida. It was also enough to silence many of the golfing pros who thought he was too young to join the professional ranks.

Tiger was tired. The pace of the PGA was exhausting. It was not only the golf but also the crowds and the constant hoopla that accompanied each tournament.

But when asked to play in the Buick Challenge Tournament in Pine Mountain, Georgia, on September 29, he agreed. He also committed to attending a special dinner honoring him as the College Golfer of the Year.

Tiger played a practice round of golf at Pine Mountain. His caddy, Mike "Fluff" Cowan, was worried by how tired Tiger looked. "Got to slow the pace," Cowan told Tiger. "You may be young, but you're still human."

At first Tiger brushed the remarks aside. But the more he thought about it, he really *was* tired. Without telling anyone, he caught a plane back to Orlando to get some rest.

People could not believe how Tiger could do such a thing. The organizer of the Buick Tournament was outraged—and let the media know it. The officials in charge of the dinner honoring Tiger were furious. "He's an ungrateful young punk!" one committee member snapped.

International Management Group, the agency handling Tiger's business affairs, tried to downplay the incident. Manager Hughes Norton explained that Tiger was mentally exhausted and that he was terribly sorry. "He wants to apologize to anyone he's inconvenienced," said Norton.

It was not enough. People wanted to hear an apology from Tiger himself. He had offended many people, and they wanted to hear from him.

Tiger delivered. He wrote personal letters of apology to every person who had planned to attend the dinner his honor. He also wrote an article for *Golf World*. He admitted to making mistakes, and reminded people that he was "only twenty years old." He said he'd reached the point where he didn't want to play golf and needed time to relax and get away from it all. "I realize now that what I did was wrong."

The grumbling died down. Reminded of how young he was, most people were willing to forgive Tiger. By the time he appeared in Las Vegas the first week in October, no mention was made of the recent situation. Tiger was relieved. He was rested and ready to thrown himself into some serious golf. Now a shining star for the Nike Corporation, he enjoyed the best of everything. He became accustomed to the first-class treatment quickly, from the Nike private jet to the penthouse suite at the MGM Grand Hotel. He only wished he could start repaying all this special attention with a win on the golf course.

Tiger's opening round was unimpressive. His score of 70 placed him in the No. 83 slot. The next day, however, he racked up a nine-under par score of 63. His position jumped, and by the final round he was tied with Davis Love III for the tournament lead. Love was a veteran golfer, and many spectators believed Tiger would collapse under the pressure of his first playoff as a pro. When he pulled a muscle and displayed a noticeable limp, Love seemed a sure winner.

But Tiger was not about to let that happen. While he practiced some tee shots, he conferred with his caddy, Mike Cowan, and his coach, Butch Harmon. Relaxed. Focused. Tiger peeled and ate a banana.

Tiger's tee shot sped down the middle of the fairway. On his second shot, he landed nicely on the green. One more shot, and in! Davis drove his opening shot into a bunker, but then he lifted his second shot onto the green. He had to sink his next shot to tie. Davis aimed and shot. The ball rolled past the hole, giving the championship to Tiger. After five PGA tournaments, he'd won his first title.

But there would be more to come.

Chapter Twelve
That Good-Looking Green Coat

There was nothing quite like the feeling of winning. Nothing at all. Somehow it instantly erased all the bad shots, all the careless swings, all the silly miscalculations. Tiger loved seeing his mom and dad smile as they ran forward to give their victory hugs. Those special moments were the best rewards.

But before the cheering of one victory died down, there was another tournament to play. Tiger managed to take third in the LaCantera Texas Open in San Antonio on October 13. Next came the Disney Classic in Orlando, Florida. Now that Tiger had a house in Orlando, it was like playing on a home court. It seemed like a good place to win again. Tiger did exactly that, posting the greatest professional start in golfing history with two wins in his first seven tournaments.

The Tour Championship was held in Tulsa, Oklahoma, on October 28. Tiger led off the first round with a par 70, then joined Earl and Tida for a night of quiet relaxation. In the middle of the night, however, Earl awoke with severe chest pains. He was rushed to St. Francis Hospital for treatment for a possible heart attack. Although he'd had heart problems before, he had not abandoned his smoking habit. By morning, Earl was feeling better and

sent Tiger back to the golf course. The rest of the tournament was a blur for him, and he ended up tied for twenty-first place.

"There are more important things than golf," Tiger told the reporters at the course. "Golf is very miniscule when it comes to your father. It was awfully hard playing, but he wanted me to come out here and do my best. I didn't want to be out here at all. Family is extremely important. It's the No. 1 priority in my life, and always will be."

Tiger slowed his pace, eager to stick around and make sure his father recuperated according to the doctors' orders. Grateful for the rest, Tiger found he did not miss playing all that much. It was enough to have *Sports Illustrated* name him Sportsman of the Year, the youngest athlete to capture the coveted award. To add icing to the cake, he was voted PGA Rookie of the Year.

Tiger started the new year by heading to La Costa Resort and Spa in Carlsbad, California. The Mercedes Championship Tournament offered $296,000 and a new Mercedes as first-prize winnings. Professional golfers poured into Carlsbad, but the final round found Tiger facing the 1996 Player of the Year, Tom Lehman, in a sudden-death match. In a drenching rain, the two golfers battled, both their games hindered by the weather.

Yet Tiger managed to avoid a disastrous pond by using a seven iron that sent his ball only six inches from the cup. Tom wasn't so lucky: His ball splashed into the water. Tiger's putt went in and he was declared the winner. He collected his check, but he gave the new Mercedes to his mom.

With the money from the Mercedes Championship, Tiger passed the $1 million dollar mark. Tiger reached that level faster than any other PGA player, and he did it in only nine pro tournaments.

At the Phoenix Open, Tiger put good use to his fame. He announced plans to form the Tiger Woods Foundation, aimed at letting inner-city kids have a chance to play golf. He kicked off the program by sponsoring his first teaching clinic. More than twenty-five hundred kids showed up to take part. "Golf has given me so much," Tiger explained. "This is my chance to give something back."

In February, Tiger got a chance to fulfill another personal dream. He flew to Thailand, his mother's homeland, to compete in the Asian Honda Classic. His arrival was covered live by all five TV networks, and fans covered him with flower necklaces at the airport. When he tried to get to the golf course, he had to ride in a helicopter because the crowds had surrounded his hotel.

Once on the golf course, Tiger blazed to an immediate victory, winning by ten strokes. He celebrated his victory by leading golf clinics for the Thai kids. Before he left, the Prime Minister of Thailand made him a citizen of the country. For once, Tiger's smile came in second in the crowd. Tida beamed even prouder than he did as she watched her son be honored.

Back in America, Tiger focused great attention on the forthcoming Masters Tournament. It would be his third appearance on the Augusta greens, and his first as a professional golfer. At least he did not have to worry about exams this time.

But Tiger did have a major concern. Earl Woods's heart required surgery. Luckily, the bypass operation in February went well, giving Tiger time to use a few tournaments as good practice sessions for the Masters in April. He was not playing his best golf, and he knew it. But being on the greens strengthened his swing and bolstered his determination.

"If his chances are based on self-confidence," one sports writer wrote, "Tiger Woods should be modeling the green jacket at the end of the tournament. However, he's up against the very best, golfers who have played this course many times and know just how to pace themselves."

Tiger was used to the media questioning his talents. There were those who thought him brash and arrogant. Memories of the Buick Classic Tournament and Tiger's walking out on those wanting to honor him the previous fall still lingered. No one denied Tiger's celebrity status, and he had certainly won tournaments. But the Masters was in a league by itself. To win the Masters demanded talent of the highest quality. Did twenty-one year-old Tiger Woods have that kind of skill?

The 1997 Masters Tournament began on April 10. So often in the past Earl Woods had followed his son from hole to hole at tournaments. Not this time. Earl was not strong enough. But Tida was willing, and Earl could watch the action from a clubhouse TV.

A chilly breeze of twenty miles per hour danced across the Augusta golf course that opening morning. However, the crowd didn't seem to notice. It was the biggest gallery to assemble for the first round in the history of the Masters. Illegal tournament badges were selling for as much as $10,000.

Tiger joined eighty-six golfers teeing off that Thursday morning. From the very beginning, his swing felt strange, tight, and rigid. Disgust gripped his face as he watched his ball careen into the pine trees to the left of the fairway. By the time he finished the 1st hole, he was one over par—a bogey. He knew he couldn't do that often if he hoped to win.

But Tiger seemed unable to break his pattern he'd started. By hole #9, he'd added three more bogeys. Drastic action was called for. As he looked out at the fairway leading to #10, he decided to shorten his swing. Swish! It worked! Tiger birdied the hole.

Yet the worst lay ahead. Holes #11, #12, and #13 at Augusta are nicknamed "Amen Corner." Deep bunkers and long hazards are tucked among flowering bushes and trees. The nickname comes from golfers claiming that all you can do on those three holes is to hit and pray.

However, Tiger did more than just that. He continued to shorten his swing, and his long shots sailed smoothly along the fairway. He chipped and putted with easy precision and unfailing accuracy. On #11, he parred. On #12 and #13, he birdied! Amen, indeed! While other golfers struggled with Amen Corner, he moved briskly forward. Despite the slow beginning, he finished with a 70, only three strokes off the lead. Most golfers would have been happy with the day's work. "I can do better," Tiger declared.

As Tiger left Friday morning to play the second round, his father had brief but clear advice. "Just kick some butt today," Earl Woods ordered, his face breaking into a big smile. Tiger nodded. He would try, that was for sure.

Tiger broke into a big smile himself when he spotted his caddie's outfit. "Fluff" Cowan wore white overalls with WOODS printed in big green letters across the back. He carried the black Titleist bag with the tiger cover wrapped over the driver.

Most of Tiger's nervousness had disappeared overnight. A few butterflies still flew around his stomach, but he felt more relaxed and at ease. His playing showed it, too. Buoyed by the big gallery, which watched his every shot and cheered him along, Tiger hit with deadeye accuracy. He took his time, not forcing anything. Gone were those nasty side shots. Gone were those bogey holes. By the end of the round, he had slipped quietly into first place, recording a dazzling 66.

A blanket of humid air covered the Augusta course on Saturday morning, April 12. The sun hid behind grey clouds, hinting of showers. "I don't think Tiger Woods ever looks up to notice the weather," one broadcaster observed. "He sees only his ball and the cup and then finds the quickest way to connect the two." There was total truth to that observation. Tiger treated his fans to a display of golf seldom witnessed on a course. No bogeys on this day, but seven birdies! Shooting an amazing seven-under-par 65, he distanced his nearest competitor by nine strokes.

No one was saying Tiger was too young for the pros anymore—no one.

The fourth and final round of Masters competition usually offers peak drama. Top golfers fight nip and tuck for the lead, with a stroke or two making all the difference in the world. This time it was different. With a nine-stroke lead, Tiger Woods was virtually invincible. When he appeared in his red polo shirt, his victory color, fans thundered their approval. "Ti-ger! Ti-ger!" The chant was deafening. Earl and Tida wore red, too, and the applause for them echoed the cheering for Tiger.

This particular Sunday featured more clouds and winds that snapped the yellow flags on the course. Tiger left the clubhouse, smiling at the huge crowd that had gathered to follow him. There was a special face—the face of a seventy-five-year-old black man. Lee Elder, the first man of color to play at the Masters, had come to see Tiger make history. "You do it, son," Elder said. Tiger nodded. He knew a lot was riding on his performance this April 12. Because of Lee Elder and people like him, Tiger was playing in the Masters.

There is no such thing as an emotional pressure gauge. If there was, it would surely have exploded inside Tiger Woods that day. Focus. Concentrate. That's easy to say with millions of people watching you from their television sets, examining your every move. Each hole, every shot were described, analyzed, evaluated. A par on #1, a birdie on #2. But there came a bogey on #5 and another on #7. But Tiger rose to the occasion, slipping into that zone, that imaginary special area removed from the earthly world, that place where there is only a golf ball, a club, a golf course, and a cup. No noise, no people. The zone.

Yes, a birdie on #8. The club felt right, the ball sailed purely and cleanly through the air. Putts dropped in. The chip shots worked. Another birdie. And another. The zone felt good. Great even. Par on this hole. Another birdie. Between shots, Tiger talked to himself. He scolded, then encouraged himself. He shook his head, then nodded. This was his world, his day.

To the very last hole, Tiger kept the world spellbound. The Masters was his, but he wanted more. He had to make par on the 18th hole to set a record. His head pounding, Tiger said a quick prayer—to the three black golfers who had played the Masters before him—and to the others who were never given the chance. One, two, three strokes and . . . in—WIN!

The crowd went wild. Tiger punched the air with his right hand, raced to Fluff Cowan, and squeezed him. Tears streaming down his face, Tiger hurried to his father and hugged him as Tida held both her men and wept too. What a day! With a score of 69 for his final day of play, Tiger had recorded the lowest Masters score ever, an eighteen-under-par 270. His closest competitor was twelve strokes back. He'd averaged 323-yard drives, 25 yards more than his runner-up. The youngest man to win the Masters, he also was the first person of color to win the championship. Golf history was rewritten that day.

Later, at a press conference, Tiger gave credit to Jackie Robinson, who had broken the color barrier in professional baseball fifty years before. Tiger hailed Charlie Sifford, Lee Elder, Ted Rhodes—the black golfers who had played the Masters before and "paved the way. . . .Those are the ones who did it."

With 1996 Masters champ Nick Faldo holding the green jacket that symbolizes the prestigious victory for the winner, Tiger slipped inside. He grinned broadly. The jacket felt good—mighty good.

Chapter Thirteen

Fore!

For years Tiger had been a celebrity, sought after by TV, radio, magazine, and newspaper reporters. But after winning the Masters Tournament in 1997, he became a media attraction of a magnitude seen seldom before. Everywhere he went, he was bombarded with questions and interview requests, his telephone rang without stopping, and letters poured in by the hundreds. "May I have your autograph?" "Could you send me your picture?" Thankfully, Michael Jordan, himself a longtime veteran of the publicity blitz, offered a helping hand and useful advice. Tiger was grateful.

And yet, just when everyone in America seemed to love Tiger, he learned of some offensive racial remarks cast in his direction by another professional golfer, Fuzzy Zoeller. Why would a fellow professional on the circuit, a friend who had struggled to master the game like he had, decide to cut him down? Zoeller was criticized by people everywhere, and he apologized, but it didn't remove the sting completely.

Then there were the expectations. Because Tiger had easily won the Masters Tournament, surely he would capture more top victories, golf watchers speculated. No one wanted that to happen more than Tiger himself. But when he competed at the U.S. Open, the British Open, the PGA Championship, and the Canadian Open, his game was

decidedly below standard. The patience and focus so long a part of his game were missing. He seemed to hurry himself, and no one was more disappointed with his performance than Tiger himself.

Of all the post-Masters encounters, Tiger's Ryder Cup experience hurt the most. Tiger headed to Spain in September as part of an elite group of U.S. golfers chosen to represent their country in international competition. The hosting Spaniards knew about Tiger's long, powerful drives. They shortened the courses for the competition, shaving fairways to make them 270 or 280 yards long. On other holes they spread new swaths of rough on the fairways. The Americans crumbled before the shrewd Spaniards, with Tiger managing to contribute only 1½ points. "I have no one to blame but myself," Tiger declared. But there were some who thought the Spaniards had acted unfairly to gain advantages over their opponents.

Despite the disappointments, Tiger was named PGA's 1997 Player of the Year. With a 69 stroke average, he managed to pull in more than $2,000,000 in tournament winnings.

But what what truly brightened Tiger's career was the success of his golfing clinics. Following the first session in Phoenix, minority kids have flocked to teaching sessions in Chicago, Los Angeles, and other cities.

"Sure, I want to be the best golfer I can be," Tiger admits. "It's always important to have dreams and to reach for them. But it's important to help others reach their dreams too, especially the kids who need the help most. You get, and you give back. That's what it's about."

The year of 1998 *was* a year of "giving back." Tiger enjoyed the time spent opening the golf clinics for kids who would never have played the game without him. On television and radio, for magazine writers and newspaper reporters, he was Paul Revere, carrying the message of golf as a game and a sport that all people could play.

On the 1998 PGA tour, Tiger's game was not up to par. He managed to win the BellSouth Classic on May 10, Mother's Day. It took a 63 on the third round to do that.

For the next nine months, Tiger hit a slump. He played, but he could not win a tournament. He made no excuses for his lackluster shooting. The smile faded a bit.

But then, on February 14, Valentine's Day, 1999, the "magic" returned. Tiger captured the Buick Invitational in San Diego by shooting an impressive 266, 22 under par, at the Torrey Hines Country Club, less than a hundred miles from Cypress, his home grounds.

"It's been a long time since I've won," the smiling Tiger declared. "I'm glad it was here in my own neighborhood, with so much of my family and so many friends here. Hopefully, my game is back. I hate to let people down who put their faith in me."

No one can know what lies ahead for Tiger Woods. One thing for sure is that he has accomplished a lot in a very short time.

Yes, for a guy who started off in life as Eldrick, he's come a long way.

Chapter Fourteen
Golf: A Brief History

How old is the sport of golf? It depends on whom you ask.

There are those who trace golf back to the Romans who occupied Great Britain in the first few centuries A.D. Using bent sticks, they swatted leather balls stuffed with feathers. The French played a similar game called *jeu de mail,* while the Dutch called their version "het kolven."

But the game of golf that Tiger Woods and about twenty million other Americans play every year is usually attributed to the Scottish. Historians find "golfe" mentioned in the 1300s, and in the following century the game was even banned by King James II, who thought his people were playing so much golf that they were neglecting their archery skills. The monarch feared invaders might attack Scotland and that his soldiers might have lost their all-important archery talents. Therefore, he outlawed golf and ordered his men back to their archery ranges. But the people continued to play on the country's natural rolling hills and oceanside sloped.

At first people played the game informally, among family and friends. In 1744, a collection of enthusiasts organized the Honourable Company of Edinburgh Golfers. The Royal and Ancient Golf Club of St. Andrews opened a decade later, winning immediate and long-lasting popularity. Rules were established for the sport, and soon golf was

being played in England and Ireland. The first British
Open Tournament was held in 1860. Scottish immigrants
carried their game to America in the mid-1800s, with John
Reid and Robert Lockhardt being given the credit for
founding the first American golf club in 1888. The two
Scotsmen set up a six-hole course on a thirty-acre plot. In
1894, they built a nine-hole course and also added a dress
code. Golfers wore knickers, plaid socks, winged collars,
jackets, and caps. The code lasted for several decades on
the "links", a Scottish word for gently rolling land.

The United States Golf Association (USGA) was formed
in 1894, with the first U.S. Open tournament held the following year. The Professional Golfer's Association (PGA)
began in 1916, and a PGA Tournament followed immediately. In 1950, the Ladies Professional Golf Association
(LPGA) was born. Most recent among major tours is the
Senior PGA, which began in 1980 and lets former PGA
golfers compete professionally against their peers.

Golf has been accused of being a sport of exclusion more
than inclusion. Although it arrived in the United States in
the late 1880s, many people could not afford to play the
game. Golf clubs were expensive, and it was also expensive
to join the private country clubs that offered courses. Those
private courses also had strict rules again people of color
playing—and women were not allowed, either.

Slowly, as other professional sports became integrated,
allowing people of any race, nationality, or sex to partici-
pate, golf followed suit. But it was not until 1975, the year
Tiger Woods was born, that a black golfer was permitted to
play in the Masters Tournament in Augusta, Georgia.
There are still places in the United States where people of
color are prevented or discouraged from playing golf.

"Golf is a sport for everyone," Tiger Woods asserts. "If
someone wishes to play, there should be no law or rule or
even any attitude that prevents that person from playing.
I was given lots of opportunities my father did not have to
succeed in this sport. Hopefully, I can open a few more
doors of opportunity for others during my career."

Chapter Fifteen
Golfer Talk at the 19th Hole

"Well, I'd better head to the driving range before I hit this course again."

"Hey, don't be discouraged. I double-bogeyed holes today that I birdied last week."

"Yeah, but you double-eagled a couple holes, too. I never did."

"We both need work. I wonder if Tiger was ever the hacker each of us was today."

"I doubt it. If he ever played the way we did, he'd be too teed off to keep playing."

Golf is a sport with its own special vocabulary. While other kids were picking up words like "apple" and "dog", young Tiger Woods was learning about "aces" and "bunkers." Here are some familiar golfing terms that will help you "ace" the "course" of golfer's chatter.

ace: to hit the golf ball from the tee into the hole using only one shot.

address: the golfer's physical position and movement before hitting the ball.

AJGA: American Junior Golf Association.

apron: the trimmed grass around the putting green.

ball line: the imaginary line between the golfer's feet and the ball.

back nine: most golfers play eighteen holes for a round of golf, the last nine holes being the back nine.

baseball grip: similar to holding a baseball bat, the golfer holds his club with the little finger of one hand touching the index finger of the other.

birdie: to score one stroke under par on any hole.

bogey: to score one stroke over par on any hole.

break: how a green curves or slopes.

bunker: an obstacle such as a sand trap placed on the golf course that makes playing more challenging.

caddie: the person who assists the golfer by carrying his golf bag, handing the golfer the club requested, providing golf balls, and offering advice and support.

chip shot: the shot used just off the putting green to get the ball closer to the hole.

club face: the bottom part of a golf club.

clubs: the instruments (woods, irons, and putters) that golfers use to hit the ball.

course: a full golf course consists of eighteen holes, planned so that the golfer can enjoy both challenge and pleasure while playing.

cup: the hole on each green into which the golfer is trying to hit the ball.

dimples: the many tiny indentations on a golf ball that increase the ball's distance and accuracy.

divot: the piece of grass the golfer tears up when he misses hitting his ball with a club.

driving range: a place where golfers go to practice hitting balls.

double bogey: a score two strokes over par on a hole.

double eagle: a score three strokes under par on a hole.

drive: the first shot a golfer takes from the tee.

eagle: a score two strokes under par on a hole.

explosion shot: a shot taken to blast out of a sand trap.

fairway: the grassy area between the tee-off area and the putting green.

flagstick: a pole topped by a flag that stands in the hole on the green so the golfer can see the target.

"Fore!": the golfer's shout before hitting the ball that warns people ahead of a forthcoming shot.

fringe: another term for apron.

front nine: the first nine holes of an eighteen-hole golf course.

gallery: the crowd that follows a particular golfer or the golfing action.

golf ball: regulation golf balls used around the world can weigh no less than 1.62 ounces and must measure at least 1.68 inches in diameter.

grain: the slight slant grass may take on a course or green.

green: the short grass near the hole where a golfer putts.

greens fee: the cost of playing golf on a public or private course.

grip: the way a golfer holds the golf club.

hacker: slang term used to describe a golfer who lacks skill or technique.

handicap: a way of adjusting a score so that golfers of different abilities can play evenly.

hazard: an obstruction such as a sand trap or a pond placed on a course to challenge golfers.

hole: the golfer's four-inch-wide, four-inch-deep target on each of a course's standard eighteen greens.

hole-in-one: hitting the ball off the tee into the hole with one drive shot (Tiger scored his first hole in one when he was six years old).

hub: imaginary chest point around which a golfer should swing the club.

irons: metal-headed golf clubs whose fronts are slanted and wedge-shaped.

irregular lie: a ball position impeded by an obstacle.

loft: the backward slant of a club face.

kiltie: the top leather flap on a golfer's shoe.

knee knocker: slang term for a short putt shot that looks easy but is not.

lie: this is the location of where the golfer's ball lands.

links: a golf course located near the ocean.

lost ball: if a golf ball cannot be located after five minutes of searching, a new one is placed where the lost ball should have landed and a one-stroke penalty is given.

LPGA: Ladies Professional Golf Association.

match play: competition between two golfers or two teams of golfers.

19th hole: after completing a round of eighteen holes, golfers often seek refreshments at a favorite spot, the "19th hole" (Tiger's favorite post-game refreshment? A Coke with cherries.).

obstruction: a hazard on the golf course unintentionally positioned.

open tournament: competition between amateur and professional golfers.

out-of-bounds: a golf ball hit outside the boundaries of the course.

par: the predetermined number of strokes needed for a golfer to tee off and reach the target hole.

penalty stroke: a stroke is added to the golfer's score if he hits the ball out-of-bound or into a hazard.

PGA: Professional Golfers' Association.

pitch shot: a high, short shot which lands and barely rolls.

preshot routine: golfer's established procedure before hitting every ball.

pro: a skilled golfer who instructs and advises and who competes professionally.

putter: a golf club used on putting green to tap or hit the ball into the cup.

putting green: the smooth grassy area surrounding each hole. *See also* green

reading the green: deciding how hard and at what angle to putt the ball.

recovery: a good shot from a bad location.

rough: the unmowed edges outside the putting green.

sand wedge: a club with a sharp wedge used to get a ball out of a sand trap.

scratch player: a talented golfer who is likely to hit par on any course.

shaft: the long middle and top of the golf club.

shank: a shot to one side that the golfer hoped to hit straight.

slice: a shot hit intentionally to sail to one side.

stance: the golfer's posture at the site of the ball.

stroke: the swing of the golf club to hit the ball.

tee: a wooden or plastic holder, one to two inches long, that holds the ball slightly off the ground.

tee shot/tee off: the first shot of each hole on a course.

tee time: the time set for beginning a round of golf.

top shot: when a golfer hit his ball high, sending it into the ground, rather than hitting it underneath so that it will sail.

triple bogey: when a golfer needs three extra strokes over par to complete a hole.

unplayable lie: when the ball's position makes it impossible to hit.

USGA: United States Golf Association.

waggle: a personal warm-up routine for a golfer.

whiff: a swing at a golf ball which misses.

woods: the largest of golf clubs, used to hit the ball long distances.

Bibliography

Edwards, Nicholas. *Tiger Woods: An American Master.* New York: Scholastic, 1997.

Gutman, Bill. *Tiger Woods: A Biography.* New York: Pocket Books, 1997.

Kramer, S. A. *Tiger Woods: Golfing to Greatness.* New York: Random House, 1997.

Rosaforte, Tim. *Tiger Woods: The Makings of a Champion.* New York: St. Martin's Press, 1997.

Woods, Earl. *Training a Tiger.* New York: HarperCollins, 1997.

Index